T0116095

ALSO BY CHARLES JOHNSON

FICTION
Soulcatcher and Other Stories
Dreamer
Middle Passage
The Sorcerer's Apprentice
Oxherding Tale
Faith and the Good Thing

PHILOSOPHY
Being and Race: Black Writing Since 1970

NONFICTION
King: The Photobiography of Martin Luther King, Jr.
(with Bob Adelman)
I Call Myself an Artist: Writings by and about Charles Johnson
(edited by Rudolph Byrd)
Africans in America
(with Patricia Smith)
Black Men Speaking
(with John McCluskey Jr.)

DRAWINGS
Half-Past Nation Time
Black Humor

TURNING
THE WHEEL

ESSAYS
ON BUDDHISM AND WRITING

CHARLES JOHNSON

Scribner

New York London Toronto
Sydney Singapore

SCRIBNER
1230 Avenue of the Americas
New York, NY 10020

Copyright © 2003 by Charles Johnson

All rights reserved, including the right of
reproduction in whole or in part in any form.

SCRIBNER and design are trademarks of
Macmillan Library Reference USA, Inc., used under license
by Simon & Schuster, the publisher of this work.

For information about special discounts for bulk purchases,
please contact Simon & Schuster Special Sales:
1-800-456-6798 or business@simonandschuster.com

Excerpt from "Culture Now: Some Animadversions, Some Laughs"
by Saul Bellow used by permission of Saul Bellow.
Excerpt from "Blue Meridian" by Jean Toomer used by permission
of Yale University.

Designed by Kyoko Watanabe
Text set in Plantin

Manufactured in the United States of America

1   3   5   7   9   10   8   6   4   2

Library of Congress Cataloging-in-Publication Data
Johnson, Charles Richard, 1948–
Turning the wheel : essays on Buddhism and writing / Charles Johnson.
p.   cm.
1. Johnson, Charles Richard, 1948– —Authorship.
2. Johnson, Charles Richard, 1948– —Religion.
3. African Americans—Authorship.
4. African Americans in literature. 5. Authorship. 6. Buddhism.
I. Title.
PS3560.O3735T8 2003
814'.54—dc21   2002044666

ISBN: 978-1-4165-7243-5

For my children
and Zack Waterfire

रूपं शून्यता शून्यतैव रूपं

Form is emptiness, emptiness is form.

THE PRAJNA-PARAMITA-HRIDAYA-SUTRA

Contents

Preface   xiii

On Buddhism

Reading the Eightfold Path   3
The Elusive Art of "Mindfulness"   34
Accepting the Invitation   42
A Sangha by Another Name   46
On the Book of Proverbs   58
A Poet of Being   68
Toro Nagashi   77

On Writing

The Role of the Black Intellectual in
   the Twenty-first Century   83
Uncle Tom's Cabin   94
The Singular Vision of Ralph Ellison   105
On *Kingsblood Royal*   112

CONTENTS

Progress in Literature 118

The Beginner's Mind 136

A Phenomenology of *On Moral Fiction* 147

"Lift Ev'ry Voice and Sing" 161

An American Milk Bottle 169

Notes 177

Acknowledgments 187

Preface

From my parents and grandparents, who were born during America's century of apartheid, from unrecorded stories I heard told by family and friends, then later from a lifetime of studying black culture, literature, and history, I came to see that if black America has a defining essence (*eidos*) or meaning that runs threadlike from the colonial era through the post–Civil Rights period, it must be the quest for freedom. This particular, eidetic sense of our collective meaning, arising out of historical conditions, and the way the Founding Fathers' ideal of freedom was inscribed with a special meaning in the souls of black folk, has shaped almost every story, essay, novel, drawing, teleplay, and critical article I've composed for the last three and a half decades. No matter whether I was writing about Frederick Douglass or James Weldon Johnson, Booker T. Washington or Harriet Beecher Stowe, Ralph Ellison or Phillis Wheatley, my sense of black life in a predominantly white, very Eurocentric society—a slave state until 1863—was that our unique destiny as a people, our duty to our predecessors who sacrificed so much and for so long, and our dreams of a life of dignity and happiness for our children were tied inextricably to a profound and lifelong meditation on what it means to be free. Truly free.

It has only been in the last thirty-seven years that black Americans have legally enjoyed the constitutional rights guaranteed to all this nation's citizens—and even then, obviously, we have numerous examples of those rights being violated. (Those few decades, I should note, are so brief, a mere blink of the eye when compared to four centuries of chattel slavery and Jim Crow segregation.) As a teenager I wondered, and I wonder still, are we free now? And if so, free to do *what?* Was our ancestors' ancient struggle for liberation realized in 1964 with the passage of the Civil Rights Act? Or in '65 with the Voting Rights Act? Or are the pointed questions of W. E. B. Du Bois in his address "Criteria of Negro Art"—"What do we want? What is the thing we are after?"—even *more* urgent today, and less easy to answer, than when African-Americans were blatantly denied basic, human rights and treated as pariahs?

Listen to Du Bois seventy-six years ago:

"If you tonight suddenly should become full-fledged Americans; if your color faded, or the color line here in Chicago was miraculously forgotten; suppose, too, you became at the same time rich and powerful;—what is it that you would want? What would you immediately seek? Would you buy the most powerful of motor cars and outrace Cook County? Would you buy the most elaborate estate on the North Shore? Would you be a Rotarian or a Lion or a What-not of the very last degree? Would you wear the most striking clothes, give the richest dinners and buy the longest press notices?" (See the essay "A Sangha by Another Name" for a longer citation from this provocative speech.)

Du Bois knew his audience well. They were members of the National Association for the Advancement of Colored People, freedom fighters all, and they heard his beautiful address in Chicago in October of 1926. He knew some of those in attendance probably thought they *would* be well satisfied—like most Americans today—with powerful automobiles, huge estates, striking clothes, rich dinners, fame, honorific titles, wealth, power, and other materialistic (and short-lived) status symbols that Du Bois dismissed as "tawdry and flamboyant." But because he was one of the founders of the NAACP, an organization devoted to a vision of the *complete advancement* of black Americans, spiritual as well as political, cultural as well as economic, Du Bois urged them not to let their ennobling journey to greater freedom degenerate into a selfish, vulgar hedonism, or a desire for the ephemeral baubles that the least enlightened members of WASP America so jealously guarded. No, I do not believe he saw freedom's fulfillment taking the form of shopping at Saks Fifth Avenue, or Andy Warhol's fifteen minutes of fame, or in the egoistic pursuit of things cheap, banal, and self-centered. For Du Bois, life's work was grander than that. Back then, he believed long-denied freedom would eventually come to black America, but with it there would be a daunting choice and the ethical challenge every human being must face. "There has been progress," he said, "and we can see it day by day looking back along blood-filled paths . . . But when gradually the vista widens and you begin to see the world at your feet and the far horizon, then it is time to know more precisely whither you are going and what you really want."

Closer to our own time, Martin Luther King Jr. offered similarly trenchant counsel to black (and all) Americans in his sermon "Rediscovering Lost Values," delivered on February 28, 1954, at Detroit's Second Baptist Church. There, just a year before the Montgomery Bus Boycott, he railed against "relativistic ethics," "pragmatism" applied to questions of right and wrong, and the "prevailing attitude in our culture," which he described as "survival of the slickest." (Does any of this seem familiar in respect to events on Wall Street in the summer of 2002?) He reminded these parishioners of that universally recognized formula for karma in Galatians 6:7 ("You shall reap what you sow"); he told them that "*all* reality hinges on moral foundations," and he moved on to critique American materialism when he said, "The great problem facing modern man is that the means *by* which we live have outdistanced the spiritual ends *for* which we live . . ."

These cultural questions, so eloquently expressed by Du Bois and King (and many others), which pose the ancient, pre-Socratic problem of how shall we live, consumed my imagination and intellectual interests from adolescence into adulthood. They kept me up late at night. They colored my perceptions of all I saw and heard in the 1960s and 1970s. They were behind my first practicing meditation when I was fourteen, falling in love with philosophy when I was eighteen, and equally behind my turn to writing novels at twenty-two. This historic devotion to freedom by black America's finest leaders also prepared me in my depths for embracing the Buddhist Dharma as the most revolutionary and civilized of possible human choices, as the logical extension of King's dream of the "beloved community," and Du Bois's "vision of what the world could be if it was really a beautiful world."

Were it not for the Buddhadharma, I'm convinced that, as a black American and an artist, I would not have been able to successfully negotiate my last half century of life in this country. Or at least not with a high level of creative productivity, working in a spirit of *metta* toward all sentient beings, and selfless service to others as a creator, teacher, husband, father, son, colleague, student, lecturer, editor, neighbor, friend, and citizen, which, in my teens, were ideals I decided I valued more than anything else. The obstacles, traps, and racial minefields faced by black men in a society that has long demonized them as violent, criminal, stupid, bestial, lazy, and irresponsible are well-documented. (See the book *Black Men Speaking*, which I coauthored with John McCluskey Jr.) And we know without needing to go into details about the difficult challenges, personal and professional, that serious literary craftsmen face at any time—and in any era—during their careers. For me, Buddhism has always been a refuge, as it was intended to be: a place to continually refresh my spirit, stay centered and at peace, which enabled me to work joyfully and without attachment even in the midst of turmoil swirling round me on all sides, through "good" times and "bad." So I am thankful for the perennial wisdom in its two-millennia-old sutras; the phenomenological insights of Shakyamuni himself into the nature of suffering, craving, and dualism; the astonishing beauty of Sanskrit, which I've been privileged to study now for five years; and the methods of different forms of meditational practice, the benefits of which fill whole libraries.

Early in the twentieth century, writer Jean Toomer recognized that Eastern philosophies and religions supported, refined, and shored up the African-American quest for freedom, providing the inner revolution necessary for completing the worldly changes our predecessors labored so hard to achieve. I believe he would be pleased to find that an increasing number of black American writers and scholars today (Thulani Davis, Jan Willis, Alice Walker, Angel Kyoto Williams) as well as entertainers (Tina Turner) are Buddhists or regularly practice some form of meditation (Trey Ellis), belong to one of its many schools, such as Theravada, Vajrayana, Ch'an, or Pure Land, or are fellow travelers such as bell hooks and Steven Barnes. (Officially, I'm registered as a member of Daigo-ji Temple, Rinzai sect, in Osaka; but the truth is that I've always been shamelessly non-sectarian.)

The number of black Dharma practitioners will, I predict, grow significantly in the twenty-first century, particularly among our scholars who want a spiritual practice not based on faith or theism and compatible with the findings of modern science; and also among our groundbreaking, innovative artists and writers whose spirit and sense of adventure cannot be contained by the traditions of the West (which, of course, they appreciate), and who hunger—as I did—to experience the world through and be enriched by as many cultural perspectives as possible. All are our human inheritance; and all, like Buddhism, have something valuable we can learn.

DR. CHARLES JOHNSON
SEATTLE, JULY 2002

On
Buddhism

Reading the Eightfold Path

The coming of Buddhism to the West may well prove to be the most important event of the Twentieth Century.

—Arnold Toynbee

To study the way is to study the self. To study the self is to forget the self. To forget the self is to be enlightened by all things. To be enlightened by all things is to remove the barriers between oneself and others.

—Dogen

All parts of the universe are interwoven with one another, and the bond is sacred.

—Marcus Aurelius

According to poet-philosopher Ashvaghosa's *Buddha-charita*, a Sanskrit poem that presents the first legendary history of the Buddha (whose name means "Awakened One"), Prince Siddhartha's experience of enlightenment came during three "watches" or phases as he sat in meditation.[1] He saw most clearly during the first watch his thousands of births and former lives. During the second watch he "beheld the whole world as in a spotless mirror"[2] (here the frequently used metaphor of the "mirror," which occurs often in Buddhist literature,[3] suggests a consciousness free of all obscuring delusions), seeing the entire universe of births and deaths driven by higher and lower merit (karma). Finally, when he entered the third watch, the Buddha saw the twelve causal links in the chain of dependent origination[4] and the Four Noble Truths. It is the fourth of these truths that will be the focus of this examination. In Ashvaghosa's poem, written in approximately 100 C.E., the Buddha expresses the Four Noble Truths in a terse, fourfold description compressed into a single sloka:

> This is pain, this also is the origin of pain in the world of living beings; this also is the stopping of pain; this is that course that leads to the stopping.[5]

What is appealing about this simple, epigrammatic statement is that it is both eidetic and a description of the empirical evidence Shakyamuni encountered in the depths of meditation. *This is pain,* he says in the First Noble Truth, where "this" refers to the entire phenomenal field of perception, to all worldly experience, which is characterized by impermanence and some form of suffering or *duhkha* (*duh,* "bad"; *kah,* "hole." Think of the hole amiddlemost a wheel, one that so poorly joins with a wagon's axle that we experience our ride through life as rough and bumpy). The second truth, *this also is the origin of pain in the world of living beings,* identifies thirst (*trishna*) or selfish desire arising from attachment as the root of *duhkha.* When he says, *This also is the stopping of pain* (the Third Noble Truth), the

Tathagata is merely reporting that he has seen how some men and women escape *duhkha*. And the fourth truth, *This is that course which leads to the stopping*, points directly to the interconnected items of the spiritual and ethical program that brings deliverance, which we call the Eightfold Path, the *Astangika-Marga*, or the *Arya Astanga Marga*.

"Just as one would examine gold through burning, cutting, and rubbing, so should monks and scholars examine my words," the Buddha said.[6] "Only thus should they be accepted; but not merely out of respect for me." He asked no one to believe or take his statements as articles of faith, or on authority. His was a philosophy that seldom, if ever, forced its adherents to proselytize. Rather, like a phenomenologist, the Buddha emphasized during his forty-five years as a teacher, "Do not go by oral tradition, by lineage of teaching, by hearsay, by a collection of scriptures, by logical reasoning, by inferential reasoning, by reflection on reasons, by the acceptance of a view after pondering it, by the seeming competence of a speaker, or because you think, 'The ascetic is our teacher.' But when you know for yourselves, 'These things are unwholesome, these things are blamable; these things are censured by the wise; these things, if undertaken and practiced, lead to harm and suffering,' then you should abandon them."[7] A testament to how many people have agreed with his critique of the human condition can be found in the fact that at one time one-third of the human race were the Buddha's students and followers;[8] and today Buddhism has 360 million adherents.

If one's own life confirms the first three Noble Truths, then the Eightfold Path ineluctably follows as the means for systematic spiritual practice. The term that precedes each step सम्यक् (*samyak*) has often been translated by Westerners as the word "right." This is not inaccurate, but it can be misleading in respect to Buddhist ontology and the ethical position that account of reality produces. Among the several meanings of *samyak* we find "rightly," "correctly," "truly," and "properly." It also means "perfect," a translation Buddhist scholar Lama Govinda preferred (as does your servant) because "perfect" suggests wholeness and completeness, and sidesteps the dualism implied by such terms as "right" and "wrong." Each of the steps on the Path has a canonical interpretation; in fact, there are different readings spread across several schools, sects, and traditions. Here I hold with the explanation of the eight steps presented in the *Mahasati-patthana Sutra* (The Greater Discourse on the Foundations of Mindfulness).[9] One learns after decades of meditation and mulling over these polysemous steps that each deepens and grows richer over one's lifetime, so that any single interpretation of, say, "Conduct" (or Action) must be seen as reflecting only a fraction of its fullness. With this in mind, the steps on the Eight-fold Path are:

Perfect View	*samyag-dristhi*	सम्यग् द्रष्टि
Perfect Thought	*samyak-sankalpa*	सम्यक् सङ्कल्प
Perfect Speech	*samyag-vach*	सम्यग् वाच्
Perfect Conduct	*samyak-karmanta*	सम्यक् कर्मन्त
Perfect Livelihood	*samyag-ajiva*	सम्यग् आजीव
Perfect Effort	*samyag-vyayama*	सम्यग् व्यायाम
Perfect Mindfulness	*samyak-smrti*	सम्यक् स्मृति
Perfect Concentration	*samyak-samadhi*	सम्यक् समाधि

Generally, in most Western translations the *Arya Astanga Marga* appears with its steps in this order. But this is not a linear movement. I will discuss them in terms of the progression above, seriatim, as most commentators do, with the caveat that the remarks about each stage will be filtered through and informed by the illuminating explanations of great teachers such as Thich Nhat Hanh. Strictly speaking, for a practitioner, the first realized steps on the Path are stages 3–5 (ethical living), followed by 6–8 (freedom from attachment), and ending with 1–2 (nonconceptual insight or wisdom).[10] Groupings and regroupings of the eight steps have consumed the energy of scholars for twenty-six hundred years. In his guide to Buddhism, John Snelling follows previous commentators when he suggests that "the path can be further subdivided into three main elements: wisdom (*panna*), morality (*sila*), and meditation (*samadhi*)."[11] (Incidentally, in different versions of the Path we find variations in the list, for example, the word *understanding* may appear instead of *view*, and *resolve* often replaces the word *thought*.) I believe *some* grouping of the eight steps can be useful. However, unlike Snelling, my preference is to group *Views* and *Thoughts* together as a "first philosophy" or the ontological side of the Path; *Speech, Action*, and *Livelihood* as a guide for civilized living in the shifting social world; and, lastly, *Effort, Concentration*, and *Mindfulness* as *praxis*, or the steps directed specifically at developing the skills and techniques, through Vipassana "insight" meditation, that shore up the other five. Naturally, all the steps presuppose, depend upon, complement, and complete each other; they are not taken one at a time, but worked on simultaneously, and as one matures with them, understanding of the steps deepens. ("Morality practiced alone can lead to involvement with other beings, as one will not have a correct view of reality as 'voidness.' Wisdom practiced alone can lead to a kind of moral and spiritual alienation from persons and things.")[12] They are all aspects, as Heidegger might say, of a particular *Dasein* or "being-in-the-world," and, by virtue of that, the eight steps must be thought about holographically or seen as prismatic sides of the same process of living. Taken as a whole, the steps of the Eightfold Path codify a profoundly human cultural vision that is in sync with the world as it is portrayed by quantum physics:[13] a vision postcultural American society at the dawn of the twenty-first century can benefit from immensely.[14]

PERFECT VIEW

In the *Mahasatipatthana Sutra*, the Buddha says, *"And what, monks, is Right View? It is, monks, the knowledge of suffering, the knowledge of the origin of suffering, the knowledge of the cessation of suffering, and the knowledge of the way of practice leading to the cessation of suffering. This is called Right View."*[15]

There is no philosophical teaching more radical, emancipatory, nonessentialistic, and empathetic than the Dharma. The Buddha's explanation of "Right View" states it demands a knowledge of the Four Noble Truths. He is concerned with but a single question, namely, why does suffering arise and how can we end it? Even more to the point is the question of *who* suffers? This is an ontological, epistemological, and moral question—the ancient problem of how one is to reconcile the One and the Many—which Buddhism addresses through the doctrine of "Dependent Origination." Thich Nhat Hanh, a master teacher of the Dharma, who was nominated by Dr. Martin Luther King Jr. for the Nobel Peace Prize, calls this ontological stance "interbeing." His eloquent explanation of this neologism appears in *Living Buddha, Living Christ:*

If we study the teachings of the Buddha and if we observe our own minds, we will find there is nothing permanent within the constituents of what we call our "self." The Buddha taught that a so-called "person" is really just five elements (*skandhas*) that come together for a limited period of time: our bodies, feelings, perceptions, mental states, and consciousness. These five elements are, in fact, changing all the time. Not a single element remains the same for two consecutive moments.

Not only is our body impermanent, but our so-called soul is also impermanent. It, too, is comprised only of elements like feelings, perceptions, mental states, and consciousness. . . . According to the teachings of the Buddha, "birth" does not exist either. Birth generally means from nothing you become something, and death generally means from something you become nothing. Before its so-called birth, this flower already existed in other forms— clouds, sunshine, seeds, soil, and many elements. Rather than birth and rebirth, it is more accurate to say "manifestation" (*vijñapti*) and "remanifestation". . . . When conditions are no longer sufficient and the flower ceases to manifest, we say the flower has died, but that is not correct either. Its constituents have merely transformed themselves into other elements, like compost and soil. We have to transcend notions like birth, death, being, and non-being. Reality is free from all notions.[16]

A lifetime of meditational practice has taught Thich Nhat Hanh that "in Buddhism there is no such thing as an individual."[17] Rather, all beings are relational and appear, as Dr. Martin Luther King Jr. put it during the Birmingham campaign in 1963, "caught in an inescapable network of mutuality, tied in a single garment of destiny. Whatever affects one directly, affects all indirectly."[18] Knowing that "all life is interrelated," this Civil Rights leader, who was surely an American Gandhi, said, "We are everlasting debtors to known and unknown men and women. . . . When we arise in the morning, we go into the bathroom where we reach for a sponge provided for us by a Pacific Islander. We reach for soap that is created for us by a Frenchman. The towel is provided by a Turk. Then at the table we drink coffee, which is provided for us by a South American, or tea by a Chinese, or cocoa by a West African. Before we leave for our jobs, we are beholden to more than half the world."[19]

Thich Nhat Hanh and Dr. King understand "Right View" as, first and foremost, a perception of reality as a *We*-relation. Even Buddhism, says Thich Nhat Hanh, "is made only of non-Buddhist elements, including Christian ones, and Christianity is made of non-Christian elements, including Buddhist ones."[20] (Which is why many "Buddhists" refuse to call themselves that, preferring instead to simply and humbly say they are students of the Dharma.) This thing we call "self" is, depending on the spiritual angle from which it is viewed, everything. And nothing.[21] It is empty (*sunyata*), possessing no essence or intrinsic reality; it is, at best, a *process* dependent each and every moment on all other beings.[22] A verb, not a noun. Or we might discuss each individual as an ever-changing "event" or "occurrence" in terms of the metaphysical position Alfred North Whitehead presents in *Process and Reality*.[23] In *The Buddhist Vision*, Alex Kennedy (Dharmachari Subhuti) expands beautifully on this insight when he writes:

> . . . everything conditioned is part of a process whose essential nature is change. Nothing, however vast and long lasting, is exempt from this universal law. . . . A tree has no reality apart from the sum of the attributes which present themselves to our senses. It is like a pointillist painting, a cloud of dancing atoms, molecules, and perhaps more sub-

tle forces in constant motion. Even these particles are, of course, not realities but are themselves compounded of smaller units which can be subdivided indefinitely. When we analyze any object, we can never come to a substance beyond which our analysis cannot penetrate. We can never find anything conditioned which has an underlying substantial reality. . . . . All things, whether subject or object, are processes linked together in an intricate network of mutual conditions. . . . The ordinary man is distracted by the bright surface of the world and mistakes this for reality.[24]

(Which, in Whiteheadean metaphysics, might be called the Fallacy of Misplaced Concreteness.)

"Perfect peace," said Shakyamuni, "can dwell only where all vanity has disappeared."[25] The word *nirvana* means "to blow out" (*nir* "out"; *vana* "blow"). In other words, when the mistaken *belief* in a separate "self" is extinguished like a candle's flame, the experiential realm of suffering and illusion, *samsara*, which so often is created and conditioned by our notions and concepts about life,[26] is replaced—as a mirage might be or the shadows in Plato's cave—because underneath it all, *underneath it all*, is a perception of being that has always been present, like dark matter, though hitherto it was obscured by the illusion of the ego. *Samsara* and *nirvana* are but two sides—or phenomenological profiles—of the same world, and which one of these two incompossible visions we experience depends on our level of consciousness. In *On the Transmission of Mind*, Huang Po insists, "Hills are hills. Water is water. Monks are monks. Laymen are laymen. But these mountains, these rivers, the whole world itself, together with sun, moon, and stars—not one of them exists outside your minds! The vast chiliocosm exists only within you, so where else can the various categories of phenomena possibly be found? Outside Mind, there is nothing."[27] For this reason, after his awakening, the poet Bunan confesses,

> *The moon's the same old moon,*
> *The flowers exactly as they were,*
> *Yet I've become the thingness*
> *Of all the things I see.*[28]

"When you are able to get out of the shell of your small self," adds Thich Nhat Hanh, "you will see that you are interrelated to everyone and everything, that your every act is linked with the whole of humankind and the whole cosmos."[29] In other words, whatever it is, it is *you*.

And what would "wrong" view be? Again, Thich Nhat Hanh provides a powerful answer:

"Regarding something that is impermanent as permanent, holding to something that is without a self as having a self, we suffer. Impermanence is the same as non-self. Since phenomena are impermanent, they do not possess a permanent identity. Non-self is also emptiness. Emptiness of what? Empty of a permanent self. Non-self means also interbeing. Because everything is made of everything else, nothing can be by itself alone. Non-self is also interpenetration, because everything contains everything else. . . . Each thing depends on all other things to be."[30]

Suffering, then, arises from the belief in a separate, unchanging "identity" for things. That is the foundation for attachment and craving. Put another way, we cling to our static ideas about things, not the fluid things themselves, which are impermanent and cannot be held on to. (Nothing can endure change yet remain unchanged.) In a universe of moment-by-moment transformations[31] all predications are risky; they *must* be highly provisional, tentative, and offered in a spirit of epistemological humility.[32] Words can be webs, making us think in terms of essences; language is all concept, but things in the world are devoid of essence, changing as we chase them. Life must always be greater than our ideas about life. For the Buddha, "Man's sensual desires are only attachments to concepts."[33] (It is not necessary, I hope, to explain how ugly and devastating are racial concepts when they are projected onto others.)

In 1997, I had the privilege and pleasure of interviewing Phra Tanat Wijitto, a young Thai abbot of skillful means in the town of Phrae near Chiang Mai. At the meditation center he was building, he explained to me that one must not be attached to even notions of Buddhism. ("I have taught you Dharma, like the parable of the raft, for getting across, for not retaining," said Shakyamuni. "You, monks . . . must not cling to right states of mind and, all the more, to wrong states of mind.")[34] Phra Tanat Wijitto was a true philosopher, which means that he had not surrendered his freedom. His focus during our two-hour dialogue was on mindfulness at all times as the heart of Buddhism; on always knowing where the mind is, on its development and freedom from what William Blake once called "mind-forg'd manacles." He insisted that all the teachers and texts, rituals and traditions, and the Three Jewels (the Buddha, Dharma, and Sangha or community of the Tathagata's followers) were simply tools for our liberation, and once one reached later stages of development, they would be left behind. (That, he predicted for me.) The rituals performed by Thai monks he saw as unfortunate but necessary "bridges" to the Dharma because people could relate to them, as a child does to a simple lesson. At higher levels of attainment, he said, a practitioner no longer created "good" or "bad" karma—there simply was no karma (or "merit") at all.[35] Moreover, for this abbot, no two odysseys to awakening were exactly the same; one progressed alone, and what one experienced could no more be transmitted to another than one can explain to a blind man the beauty of an orchid. Put simply, to follow the Dharma is to live without a net. Or solid ground. Without a place to rest. Without mind-created or language-created constructs. (I was reminded by this of philosopher Ludwig Wittgenstein's advice, "Don't explain, *look!*") Furthermore, this gentle, percipient monk understood that Buddhism was synonymous with creativity. It, too, was subject to change, process, and transformation. He saw America as good for my practice of the Dharma because in this "developed" country, as he put it, we have more time for the practice of meditation and studying the sutras than do the far poorer people of Thailand. Some of the laity, he told me, will grasp the Buddha-dharma in seven days, others in seven months, and still others will fail to understand it after seven years, if at all.

The Dharma is, if nothing else, a call for us to live in a state of radical freedom. It is not a Way for anyone who denies the fact that from the moment of our birth we have been dying, and that one day this universe itself will experience proton death—all that men and women have done will be as if it never was[36]— black holes will eventually evaporate into photons, leaving only a Void, from which (perhaps) another, different universe will arise.[37] In *The Diamond Sutra,* we are told, "Those who find consolation in limited doctrines involving the conception of an ego entity, a personality, a being, or a separated individuality, are unable to accept, receive, study, recite, and openly explain this discourse."[38] That sutra ends with this verse:

> *Thus shall ye think of all this fleeting world:*
> *A star at dawn, a bubble in a stream;*
> *A flash of lightning in a summer cloud,*
> *A flickering lamp, a phantom, and a dream.*[39]

PERFECT THOUGHT

"And what," asked the Buddha, *"is Right Thought? The thought of renunciation, the thought of non-ill-will, the thought of harmlessness. This, monks, is called Right Thought."*[40]

In Sanskrit, the word *sankalpa* can mean both "thought" and "resolve." I imagine that those who prefer *resolve* do so to highlight the fact that harmlessness (*ahimsa*) toward all sentient beings necessarily follows from the understanding that we are never involved in "I/Thou" or "I/It" relationships, but instead only in "I am Thou" relationships. If all sentient beings are caught in a mutually interdependent process of manifestation and remanifestation, then, according to the *Visuddhimagga,* "Bhikkus, it is not easy to find a being who has not formerly been your mother . . . your father . . . your brother . . . your sister . . . your son . . . your daughter."[41] All clearly want the same two things that we do: to find happiness and avoid suffering. Toward all sentient beings there is but one proper response: compassion and loving kindness (*metta*).

The Buddha was both an *arhat* who, in the Hinayana tradition, attained *nirvana* and will not return to the wheel of birth and death; and he was a *bodhisattva*, one in the Mahayana tradition who transcended *samsara*, but—due to his compassion—renounced full immersion in *nirvana* in order to work indefatigably for the salvation of all sentient beings. For the Dharma follower, even the "desire" for liberation from suffering can become a trap, a form of attachment, an instance of dualism ("I am not free; I wish to be free"), and so he must "let go" that craving as well. Better to simply attend mindfully to the "here" and "now," helping to reduce the *himsa* all around him when the occasion to do so arises, and to practice with no thought of personal "reward" or "gain." His resolve is expressed in the ancient

Bodhisattva Vows found in most, if not all, Mahayana sects and schools:

> *Sentient beings are numberless;*
> *I take a vow to save them.*
> *The deluding passions are inexhaustible;*
> *I take a vow to destroy them.*
> *The Gates of Dharma are manifold;*
> *I take a vow to enter them.*
> *The Buddha-way is supreme;*
> *I take a vow to complete it.*[42]

as well as in Shantideva's *A Guide to the Bodhisattva's Way of Life:*

> *First of all I should make an effort*
> *To meditate upon the equality between self and others:*
> *I should protect all beings as I do myself*
> *Because we are all equal in (wanting) pleasure and (not*
>   *wanting) pain.*
>
> *Hence I should dispel the misery of others*
> *Because it is suffering, just like my own,*
> *And I should benefit others*
> *Because they are sentient beings, just like myself.*
>
> *When both myself and others*
> *Are similar in that we wish to be happy,*
> *What is so special about me?*
> *Why do I strive for my happiness alone?*[43]

PERFECT SPEECH

"And what, monks, is Right Speech? Refraining from lying, refraining from slander, refraining from harsh speech, refraining from frivolous speech. This is called Right Speech."[44]

There are several observations to make about *samyag-vach*, the first being that in the "Sutra of Forty-two Sections," the Buddha sharpened this injunction, saying, "Lie not, but be truthful, and speak truth with discretion, not so as to do harm, but in a loving heart and wisely. Invent not evil reports, neither do ye repeat them. Carp not, but look for the good sides of your fellow beings, so that you may with sincerity defend them against their enemies. . . . Waste not the time with empty words, but speak to the purpose or keep silence. Covet not, nor envy, but rejoice at the fortunes of other people. . . . Cherish no hatred, not even against your slanderer, nor against those who do you harm, but embrace all living beings with kindness and benevolence. . . . He must not flatter his vanity by seeking the company of the great. Nor must he keep company with persons who are frivolous and immoral. . . . He must not take delight in quarrelous disputations or engage in controversies so as to show the superiority of his talents, but be calm and composed."[45]

Consider Shakyamuni's admonition *Waste not the time with empty words* in light of how in America, and elsewhere in the world, we daily abuse the power of language, diminish and trivialize it when we use talk as merely another form of entertainment, or a way to amuse ourselves and others; to pass the time or simply fill the silence that envelopes us and is the ground and precondition for speech. Lying, slander, and harsh speech are obvious ways that we hurt others, wounding them with words. But as Martin Heidegger points out in *Being and Time*, "idle talk" is equally a violation of the being of language, which at its best is the means for dislodging consciousness from calcified, prefabricated thinking and disclosing truth.

"Discourse," says Heidegger, "has the possibility of becoming idle talk. And when it does, it serves not so much to keep Being-in-the-world open for us in an articulated understanding, as rather to close it off, and cover up the entities within-the-world. To do so, one need not aim to deceive. . . . The fact that something has been said groundlessly, and then gets passed along in further retelling, amounts to perverting the act of disclosing. . . . Thus, by its very nature, idle talk is a closing-off, since to go back to the ground of what is talked about is something which it *leaves undone*."[46]

Not only do we live in a culture where "idle talk" covers up and conceals interbeing, but also one in which different forms of violence have become entertainment and recreation. Violence is not only physical. It is also psychological and verbal. It begins in the mind. All my life I've wondered what would it be like to live in a society where, instead of men and women insulting and tearing each other down, people in their social relations, and even in the smallest ways, held the highest intellectual, moral, creative, and spiritual expectations for one another. One step toward achieving that is contained in an old Buddhist idea that urges us to momentarily detain all thought at three "gates"—or questions—before it crystallizes into speech. The three gates are "Is what we are about to say *true?* Will it cause no *harm?* And is it *necessary?*" If all three answers are in the affirmative, then (and only then) have we realized *samyag-vach*.

Do some languages facilitate better than others the intuition of interbeing? Kobo Daishi (774–835 C.E.), founder of the Shingon school of Japanese Buddhism, privileged Sanskrit, believing that only this language could express the meaning of the mantras used in Shingon.[47] Clearly, there is a sharpening of one's intellectual understanding of the Buddhadharma if one reads Sanskrit, which means "refined" or "language brought to formal perfection."[48] But Sanskrit offers more than linguistic accuracy. It is the language of mantra (*man* "mind"; *tra* "refuge" or "protection"). Of the Dharma. In its almost calculus-like exactitude, Sanskrit's rule for *sandhi* (the harmonizing of sounds) allows each syllable spoken to blend almost seamlessly into the next. When translating Sanskrit, you think and sing the world differently. Henry David Thoreau, the first translator of the Lotus Sutra into English,[49] praised its oldest texts: "What extracts from the Vedas I have read fall on me like the light of a higher and purer luminary which describes a loftier course through a purer stratum. . . . The Vedas contain a sensible account of God."[50] Joseph Campbell called it "the great spiritual language of the world."[51] One of America's highly respected Sanskrit teachers, Vyaas Houston, says, "Even the earliest stages of learning Sanskrit require the one-pointedness of Yoga. Sanskrit tests and strengthens the skill of Yoga, and gradually it provides Yoga with its language, manuals, and maps for mastery."[52]

What is remarkable is that sometimes a Sanskritist can literally see interbeing in the slokas that comprise texts such as the many-splendored *Bhagavad Gita* or the sobering, veil-lifting *Astavakra Samhita,* a work in the Advaita Vedanta tradition. I said earlier that language is being; life is becoming. Yes. But now and then, with Sanskrit, language mirrors becoming and process. In the *Astavakra Samhita,* in chapter 15 ("The Knowledge of the Self"),[53] the fourteenth verse declares, "You alone appear as whatever you perceive. Do bracelets, armlets, and anklets appear different from gold?" In Devanagari script, that final line is written as:

कटकांगदनूपुरम्

When "bracelet" (कटकः), "armlet" (अंगदं), and anklet (नूपुरः) combine as a *dvandva* (or *samahara*) compound through *sandhi*, they are no longer three separate "events" but rather the manifestation of an entirely new form (*rupam*),[54] which is experienced, phenomenologically, as such. Here, grammar perfectly mirrors the cosmology of Hinduism, and additional examples for the startling, shape-shifting play of words in Sanskrit, interwoven entities combining and recombining endlessly, can easily be found in the *Bhagavad Gita*.[55]

In Sanskrit, the spoken word is holy, far removed from the "idle talk" of Heidegger's complaint. Each is energy unleashed. Each is a bridge between subjectivities. Each can potentially create a public, shared space in which we can raise the American Sangha—just as "wrong" speech can destroy that possibility. Preserving this creative, primordial power is, I believe, what the Buddha intended, at least in part, when he described this third step on the Path.

PERFECT CONDUCT

"And what, monks, is Right Action? Refraining from taking life, refraining from taking what is not given, refraining from sexual misconduct. This is called Right Action."[56]

The Eightfold Path is more process than end product. It is like climbing a mountain in a circular, upwardly spiraling fashion, finding oneself forever returned to the same spot but at a different level. Thus, both the *bodhisattva* and the novice practitioner move through this splintered, relative-phenomenal world, where things arise and are unraveled in a fortnight. But it is *how* they move and act in the world that is important. "Doing" for the Dharma follower is an example of disinterested, deontological ethics, which, like that found in Kantian philosophy, is "interested in the act, never the fruit."[57] In the *Astasahasrika-prajñaparamita*[58] ("The Perfection of Wisdom"), we learn:

> . . . a bodhisattva . . . should behave equally to all sentient beings. He should produce thoughts that are fair to all sentient beings. He should handle others with thoughts that are impartial, that are friendly, that are favorable, that are helpful. He should handle others with thoughts that are nonconfrontational, that avoid harm, that avoid hurt, that avoid distress. He should handle others, all sentient beings, using the understanding of a mother, using the understanding of a father, the understanding of a son and the understanding of a daughter. . . . He should be trained to be the refuge of all sentient beings. In his own behavior he should renounce all evil. He should give gifts, he should guard morality, he should exercise patience, he should exert vigor, he should enter into contemplation, and he should master his wisdom! He should consider dependent origination backwards and forwards, and he should instigate, encourage, and empower that in others.[59]

The strict, daily regimen of monks is far from easy, but how much more demanding is the life of the householder with half a hundred duties barnacled to his (or her) life, the *upasaka* and *upasika* (male and female Buddhist lay adherents) who strive to follow the Buddhadharma, not in a secluded monastery where the residents are free from worldly temptations, but in the roiling chaos of quotidian affairs—raising children; honoring parents, spouse, and ancestors; supporting colleagues and coworkers (and students) around the world in an ever-widening circle of giving. In other words, by transforming *samsaric* means for *nir-*

vanic ends. Living and working in *kamadhatu* (the world of desire) *and* being "capable of perceiving both unity and multi-plicity without the least contradition between them."[60] This is, I think, the greatest of spiritual (and moral) challenges. For the "bodhisattva . . . is not one to give weight to gain, honor, and fame. He is not to give weight to fancy robes . . . a nice dwelling place. . . . He is not full of envy and meanness. . . . His under-standing is deep. He eagerly hears teaching from others, and he incorporates all that teaching into the perfection of wisdom. He incorporates all the worldly arts and profession through their inherent nature, thanks to the perfection of wisdom."[61] (Can any-one doubt that Buddhists make the best employees and bosses?)

One of the perennially enchanting documents of Ch'an (Zen) Buddhism is the "Ten Oxherding Pictures," which inspired my second novel, *Oxherding Tale* (1982). These draw-ings depict the spiritual stages of Zen development that lead to enlightenment by portraying the search of a young herdsman for his lost ox (self). Each illustration is followed by commen-tary in prose and verse. The ten stages shown are (1) Seeking the Ox; (2) Finding the Tracks; (3) First Glimpse of the Ox; (4) Catching the Ox; (5) Taming the Ox; (6) Riding the Ox Home; (7) Ox Forgotten, Self Alone; (8) Both Ox and Self Forgotten; (9) Returning to the Source; and (10) Entering the Marketplace with Helping Hands.[62] It is this final panel that speaks signifi-cantly to the question of Perfect Conduct.

The version of the Oxherding Pictures important for this discussion was created in 1150 C.E. by Zen master K'uo-an Shih-yuan (Kakuan Shien in Japanese). Some earlier versions of the Oxherding Pictures offered only five or eight drawings, usu-ally ending with an empty circle (Both Ox and Self Forgotten),[63] which fit nicely the *arhat* ideal of Theravada Buddhism. "This implied," says Philip Kapleau, "that the realization of Oneness (i.e., the effacement of every conception of self and other) was the ultimate goal of Zen. But Kakuan, feeling this to be incomplete, added two more pictures beyond the circle to make it clear that the Zen man of the highest spiritual development lives in the mundane world of form and diversity and mingles with the utmost freedom among ordinary men, whom he inspires with his compassion and radiance to walk in the Way of the Buddha."[64] Shih-yuan's final, tenth picture is accompanied by this commentary:

10 / **Entering the Marketplace with Helping Hands** / The gate of his cottage is closed and even the wisest cannot find him. His mental panorama has finally disappeared. He goes his own way, making no attempt to follow the steps of earlier sages. Carrying a gourd, he strolls into the market; leaning on his staff, he returns home. He leads innkeepers and fishmongers in the Way of the Buddha.[65]

Kapleau's gloss on the commentary of this tenth image deserves examination:

In ancient China gourds were commonly used as wine bottles. What is implied here therefore is that the man of the deepest spirituality is not adverse to drinking with those fond of liquor in order to help them overcome their delusion. . . . In Mahayana Buddhism . . . the man of deep enlightenment (who may be and often is the layman) gives off no 'smell' of enlightenment, no aura of 'saintliness'; if he did, his spiritual attainments would be regarded as still deficient. Nor does he hold himself aloof from the evils of the world. He immerses himself in them whenever necessary to emancipate men from their follies, but without being sullied by them himself. In this he is like the lotus, the symbol in Buddhism of purity and perfection, which grows in mud yet is undefiled by it.[66]

Often we hear that the attainment of Oneness, or being awakened, is "nothing much" (for the belief in separateness was a chimera in the first place).[67] Like Bunan, the Oxherder discovers that "The moon's the same old moon / The flowers exactly as they were." He will take a drink. And perhaps eat meat. But to none of this is he attached. Nor does he crave them. Like the abbot I met in Thailand, he does not fret about "good" or "bad" karma, because in his conduct all he is capable of are acts in accordance with *ahimsa*, which he does not name or judge as "good," no more than the lotus bothers to name the natural act of its efflorescence. And the Oxherder has a sense of humor and irony. How could he not? He knows that, despite all he has attained through a lifetime of practice, he is still an embodied being and, as such, will experience until the day of his death a residual stain of dualism, a tincture of *samsara*, and traces of suffering, which he recognizes when they arise in his consciousness. All that he "lets go," and when he dies, falling like a raindrop back into the sea,[68] it is unlikely he will return (or return too often) on the Wheel of remanifestation. He is, in a sense, a refugee—homeless and groundless.[69] He watches the ceaseless play of his thoughts, but is not naive enough to believe there is a thinker. (For a Buddhist, Descartes asserted but he did not prove his claim "I think, therefore I am," because all that one can empirically verify is that "There is thinking going on.") He is alone *with* others[70] who are also refugees or tourists with no solid basis for security, and nothing permanent in this world. He pilgrimages through the Marketplace (the realm that turns on four, dualistic pairs of opposites: "getting and losing, disrepute and fame, blame and praise, happiness and suffering")[71] with fearlessness, probity, desirelessness (*nishpriha*), transcendent joy, and he delights in the *suchness* of everyday things:

> *How wonderful, how marvelous!!*
> *I fetch wood, I carry water!*[72]

To the innkeepers and fishmongers, the Oxherder appears, in one sense, as nothing special, with no sanctimonious stink of self-righteousness on him since all sentient beings have Buddha-nature and dwell in "an inescapable network of mutuality." But through his example—his compassion toward all beings, his gentle speech, and his unshakable peace and happiness—he points them toward their own possibilities.

PERFECT LIVELIHOOD

"And what, monks, is Right Livelihood? Here, monks, the . . . disciple, having given up wrong livelihood, keeps himself by right livelihood."[73]

The Buddha counsels his followers to avoid occupations that produce harm. He is referring to obvious evils such as dealing in slaves, producing weapons or intoxicating drinks, all activities that are as much a part of our world as they were of his. Few, I think, would deny that in the modern world humankind has inventively expanded upon the wealth of deeds that damage or destroy sentient beings, ranging from fast-vanishing animal species to the environment. Our Oxherder is free to find employment almost *any*where, provided the work he chooses doesn't violate what he has learned about Perfect Conduct and Perfect Speech, compassion and the Bodhisattva Vows.

Yet because so many people are involved in "wrong" livelihoods, many Buddhists understand that "evil must be combatted by nonviolent means. We must battle against everything which drags men down, using criticism, exhortation, influence, and whatever means are ethically sound and cause no harm to others."[74]

In other words, the flip side of avoiding a livelihood that harms is embracing a livelihood that heals. In his workshops, Thich Nhat Hanh distributes a page containing what he calls "The Five Mindfulness Trainings." The first of these declares, "Aware of the suffering caused by the destruction of life, I vow to cultivate compassion and learn to protect the lives of people, animals, plants, and minerals. I am determined not to kill, not to let others kill, and not to condone any act of killing in the world, in my thinking, and in my way of life." The third vow goes further: "I will respect the property of others, but I will *prevent* others from profiting from human suffering or the suffering of other species on earth." (Italics mine.)

To put this another way, followers of the Buddhadharma, fully aware of impermanence, dualism, and relativity, yet also aware of the ubiquity of suffering, are obliged at some point to oppose the origins of *duhka* in the social world. They will, I believe, share the dreams stated by Dr. Martin Luther King Jr. in his Nobel Prize acceptance speech in 1964, where he said, "Civilization and violence are antithetical concepts. . . . Nonviolence is the answer to the crucial political and moral question of our time. . . . The foundation of such a method is love. . . . I have the audacity to believe that peoples everywhere can have three meals a day for their bodies, education and culture for their minds, and dignity, equality, and freedom for their spirits. I believe that what self-centered men have torn down men other-centered can build up."[75]

To work for *this*, to find an occupation that realizes *this*, is to fulfill the step called Perfect Livelihood.

PERFECT EFFORT

"And what, monks, is Right Effort? Here, monks, a monk rouses his will, makes an effort, stirs up energy, exerts his mind, and strives to prevent the arising of unarisen evil, unwholesome mental states. He rouses his will . . . and strives to overcome evil, unwholesome mental states that have arisen. He rouses his will . . . and strives to produce unarisen wholesome mental states. He rouses his will, makes an effort, stirs up energy, exerts his mind, and strives to maintain wholesome mental states that have arisen, not to let them fade away, to bring them to greater growth, to the full perfection of development. This is called Right Effort."

The first sentence of the *Dhammapada* declares, "All that we are is the result of what we have thought: it is founded on our thoughts, it is made up of our thoughts. If a man speaks or acts with an evil thought, pain follows him, as the wheel follows the foot of the ox that draws the wagon."[76] Of all the world's religions and philosophies, Buddhism is the most optimistic. It places creative control over the direction of our lives in our hands. You are your own master. Moment by moment, whatever suffering, joy, or peace we experience is always the direct result of our past and present decisions. If we wish to be free, we must liberate ourselves. No one can do this for us. No one can lead us. Or place insurmountable obstacles in our way. According to the *Dhammapada*, "Those who are thoughtless are as if dead already."[77] By contrast, "He who is earnest and meditative obtains ample joy" because he knows, "it is good to tame the mind, which is difficult to hold in and flighty, rushing wherever it listeth; a tamed mind brings happiness."[78]

It is good to tame the mind.

As any teacher can tell you, the minds of most students are— well, *un*tamed. Their minds, and those of most people, behave like Vivekananda's famous "drunken monkey," intoxicated with desire, consumed by pride and jealousy, trigger-happy with snap judgments, burdened by miscellaneous "likes" and "dislikes," his turbulent "mental panorama" causing him to leap uncontrollably from one thought and feeling to the next, dizzied by the elixir of powerful emotions banging and knocking through him like something trying to break out from inside. For him, the ego favors a bump in a carpet—push it down in one place and it pops up in another. The monkey does not know *how* to behave otherwise and is to be pitied. One tragedy of American education, in my view, is that from elementary school through postdoctoral programs, we place a staggering amount of intellectual, noematic content before the minds of our students, content covering all aspects of the universe, but we never teach them how to control the experienced world at its source: the noetic instrument[79]—the mind—that both receives this vast gift of information *and* makes experience possible.[80]

Disciplining the mind first involves *effort* directed toward developing the power of sustained concentration (*dharana*), followed by meditation (*dhyana*). The Buddha makes clear that this practice involves stupendous will and work, for no worldly opponent is as formidable as one's own "monkey mind."

But where, in terms of practice, should we begin?

PERFECT MINDFULNESS

"And what, monks, is Right Mindfulness? Here, monks, a monk abides contemplating body as body, ardent, clearly aware and mindful, having put aside hankering and fretting for the world; he abides contemplating feelings as feelings . . . ; he abides contemplating mind as mind . . . ; he abides contemplating mind-objects

as mind-objects, ardent, clearly aware and mindful, having put aside hankering and fretting for the world. This is called Right Mindfulness."[81]

The problem of life is, to a great degree, the problem of attention. Of *listening*, which is one of the attributes of love. Therefore, all steps on the Eightfold Path refer and return to the practice of Mindfulness. It is the root and fruit of the Dharma, a method for meditation taught by Shakyamuni himself. "Whoever, monks, should practice [this method] for just one week may expect one of two results: either Arahantship in this life or, if there should be some substrate left, the state of a Nonreturner."[82] In what is known as Vipassana or "insight" meditation, a practitioner applies the forceps of his attention to one of the activities closest to him—the in-and-out flow of his breath. (Once, when my daughter was five or so, she saw me sitting and referred to my practice as "medicating," and in a sense she was right; each meditation is both medicinal and the opportunity to hold a funeral for the ego.) But this is no easy task. Try, if you can, to focus on your breath and nothing else for five minutes. I doubt that you can do this. After a few seconds the labile mind will wander from following the breath to memories, projections for future plans, thoughts, reveries, and the entire "mental panorama" that leaves only 30 percent of our lives lived in the present moment, the *here* and *now*. All too often, 30 percent of conscious life is wasted by our mind's dwelling on events in the unrecoverable past; another 30 percent is lost preliving the future. Put simply, we are seldom fully 100 percent in the present. Giving the mind something to hold on to in order to keep it fully in the *here* and *now* favors a technique used by every mahout who must train his elephant not to swing its trunk wildly in all directions, which is, of course, dangerous for anyone who gets in the way. The mahout gives the elephant a stick to grasp, and that both calms and centers its attention. In Vipassana, the "stick" we try to hold on to is our breathing itself.

This one-pointed grasping is sometimes called *ekagrata* (*eka*, "one"; *grah*, "to seize or grasp"), and sometimes *ananya-cheta* (*ananya*, "exclusively devoted to"; *cheta*, "meditation" or "mind"). Whenever the mind veers away from the in-and-out rhythm of breathing, the practitioner dispassionately observes its wanderings, then gently brings it back. He does not scold himself for his lapses. His effort is concentrated on radical attentiveness to detail, physical and psychological, a focus directed at achieving complete awareness—right down to the most subtle nuances and modulations—of what appears before consciousness as he sits. (Was this breath long or short, hot or cold? Are my shoulders straight or slumped?) In due course, he understands why the Buddha said, "Whatever is subject to arising must also be subject to ceasing." Suffering is no exception to this law.[83]

Now, watch:

The practitioner sees that, like the rising and falling movement of his breath, each thought, emotion, feeling, and ache in his back is impermanent, changing like everything else in the world, and will pass away like clouds moving across the sky if he attends to them long enough. It becomes increasingly easy, he discovers, to "let go" what the Buddha calls "evil, unwholesome mental states" and use his will to "maintain wholesome mental states that have arisen." In Vipassana he does not interpret evanescent mental phenomenon as they arise. It is quite enough to simply recognize the brief, flicker-flash passing of a feeling *as* no than more a feeling, a transitory mind-created object *as* no more than a mind-object. "With the eye of Wisdom," says Alex Kennedy, "he sees that . . . He himself is Empty, all other things are Empty. He sees that the basic nature of all reality is that ungraspable oneness which is called Emptiness. . . .

It is not a blank nothingness but such a plentitude that all our ordinary categories of thought diminish and belittle it."[84]

This impermanance recognized through Mindfulness is an antidote for intellectual arrogance, and it brings with it a bracing moral discovery. The challenge of always "being good" is, obviously, daunting. Who can *always* behave morally? Is it not, after all, as impossible to control the mind as it would be to harness the wind? What the practitioner realizes is that he need not worry about "always," because as Swami Budhananda says so beautifully in *The Mind and Its Control*, "We must clearly see that every moment is only *this moment*. If we have taken care of this moment, we have taken care of our entire future. . . . The future is nothing but Maya. . . . The challenge of the spiritual life is very simple: to be good, truly moral and master of ourselves for only this moment. What time is there outside this moment, that we should worry about it?"[85] This moment *here* and *now* is all that we are given or responsible for.[86] "Unwholesome mental states" will appear, rise and pass away like "a star at dawn, a bubble in a stream, a flash of lightning in a summer cloud, a flickering lamp, a phantom, and a dream," if we do not sustain them by clinging and just let them disappear.

The direct result of this practice, according to Kennedy, is that our Oxherder is "in full possession of his own body: he knows what his posture is, what he is doing and the direction and purpose of his movements. . . . He is aware of his emotions. He knows whether he feels greed, hatred or delusion, or metta, generosity, and clarity. He knows what he thinks: what thoughts and images are passing through his mind. And he knows where those thoughts have come from. He is able to distinguish what in his mind is simply the product of his past conditioning and what is genuinely creative. . . . He is able to rise to challenges and deal with them with imagination and resourcefulness. . . . He sees things with the eye of aesthetic appreciation, not of egotistical appropriation. He is profoundly moved by beauty in nature and in art."[87]

Mindfulness is not only practiced when sitting. It can—and should—be brought to each and every one of our activities, regardless of how humble they might be. When walking, eating, taking out the garbage, or talking, the Dharma urges us to practice a complete and dispassionate awareness of where we are and what we are doing. Such practice is transformative, as proven by seventy-eight-year-old S. N. Goenka, one of the world's foremost Vipassana teachers, who has taught its techniques to hundreds of thousands of people, among them hardened criminals at Tihar Jail, "India's largest and most notorious prison."[88] Recidivism dropped among inmates guided through Vipassana by Goenka, at prisons both in India and in America.

"This," Goenka says, "is universal. You sit and observe your breath. You can't say this is Hindu breath or Christian breath or Muslim breath. Knowing how to live peacefully or harmoniously—you don't call this religion or spirituality. It is nonsectarian."

The Dharma and its practice need not be "called" anything. Wisdom practices are the property of no single religion or philosophy.

RIGHT CONCENTRATION

"And what, monks, is Right Concentration? Here, a monk, detached from sense desires, detached from unwholesome mental states, enters and remains in the first jhana, which is thinking and pondering, born of detachment, filled with delight and joy. And with the subsiding of thinking and pondering, by gaining inner tranquillity and oneness of

mind, he enters and remains in the second jhana, which is without thinking and pondering, born of concentration, filled with delight and joy. And with the fading away of delight, remaining imperturbable, mindful, and clearly aware . . . he enters the third jhana. And having given up pleasure and pain, and with the disappearance of former gladness and sadness, he enters and remains in the fourth jhana, which is beyond pleasure and pain, and purified by equanimity and mindfulness. This is called Right Concentration. And that, monks, is called the way of practice leading to the cessation of suffering."[89]

In the dialectic of *samsara* and *nirvana*, the experiential realms of ignorance and wakefulness, the dreamworld of *samsara* is logically prior to and necessary for the awakening to *nirvana*. Gunapala Dharmasiri argues that this is the stance of Tantric Buddhism:

"If Samsara is only a mental construct, a maya, the Tantrics ask, why should we be scared of our own creations or dreams? . . . What is necessary is to master and get out of the dream. Once we get out of the dream, we will wake up to the Nirvana, which is this world itself. . . . We make a Samsara out of Nirvana through our conceptual projections. Tantrics maintain that the world is there for two purposes. One is to help us to attain enlightenment. As the world is, in fact, Nirvana, the means of the world can be utilized to realize Nirvana, when used in the correct way."[90]

For the approximately 2 million Buddhists in America, the Eightfold Path is a map for the Way. But, like any map, it merely sketches the terrain *bodhisattvas* have traversed for two and a half millennia, leaving open for each follower of the Dharma an adventure of discovery and service: a genuinely creative journey through the mystery of being, which with each step leads to ineffable joy.

The Elusive Art of "Mindfulness"

As a student wrote: If one is trying to do something really well, one becomes, first of all, interested in it, and later absorbed in it, which means that one forgets oneself in concentrating on what one is doing. But when one forgets oneself, oneself ceases to exist, since oneself is the only thing which causes oneself to exist.

—Christmas Humphreys,
Concentration and Meditation

For more than twenty years I've kept this intriguing statement about the relationship between self and work pasted to the writing desk in my study to remind me—as a Buddhist and creator, husband and father, teacher and citizen—that concentration *(dharana)* not only is traditionally the first stage in the ancient practice of formal meditation *(dhyana)*, but also expresses itself in the one-pointedness of mind required for the doing well of *any* worldly activity, including the lifelong labor of writing. In fact, as someone who has been publishing stories for thirty-eight years, practicing meditation for twenty-three, and studying Eastern philosophy for thirty-two, I cannot help but marvel sometimes at the striking analogues between meditation and moments of intense creative inspiration, and how both overlap in my life and literary offerings.

Yet it matters not at all if the activity we're talking about is writing a novel, preparing dinner, teaching a class, serving tea, or simply walking, the spiritual point is everywhere and always the same: any action is performed best and most beautifully, especially unpleasant tasks, when the actor practices what Buddhists call "mindfulness"; when he is wholly and selflessly aware of every nuance in the activity and immersed in it; when he gets the gossamer-thin illusion of the self out of the way and, in a delightful modulation of consciousness and temporality, experiences only the *here* and the *now*, with no concern at all for the unrecoverable past or a future that never comes.

But, sadly, for most Americans, that kind of concentration and nonattachment *(vairagya)* is elusive, particularly in a TV-oriented and movie-drenched carnival culture that produces a short attention span in a population relentlessly bombarded by trivial distractions and weighted down by ego baggage—elusive, that is, until one learns to carefully observe the behavior of the mind and make it one's servant.

No one knows better than those who regularly practice some form of meditation that we are seldom, if ever, the complete master of our mind's operations, thoughts, and cravings. For that reason, early in the canonical Buddhist text *The Dhammapada*, we find this observation:

> *Hard to hold down,*
> *nimble,*
> *alighting wherever it likes:*
> *the mind.*

Its taming is good.
The mind well-tamed
brings ease.

At first glance, one thinks: What a preposterous challenge! You might as well try to tame the wind. In *Raja-Yoga*, the nineteenth-century philosopher-teacher Vivekananda employed a popular, East Indian metaphor for the mind's contumacy, one found sprinkled throughout Hindu and Buddhist literature, to describe this very quotidian dilemma:

> There was a monkey, restless by its own nature, as all monkeys are. As if that were not enough, someone made him drink freely of wine, so that the monkey became still more restless. Then a scorpion stung him. When a man is stung by a scorpion, he jumps about for a whole day; so the poor monkey found his condition worse than ever. To complete his misery a demon entered into him. What language can describe the uncontrollable restlessness of that monkey? The human mind is like that monkey, incessantly active by its own nature; then it becomes drunk with the wine of desire, thus increasing its turbulence. After desire takes possession comes the sting of the scorpion of jealousy of the success of others, and last of all the demon of pride enters the mind, making it think itself of all importance. How hard to control such a mind.

Vivekananda's humorous yet horrifyingly recognizable "monkey mind" is, obviously—*unclear*. (As cartoonist David Bergman put it, "A mind is a terrible thing to watch.") It is a mind clouded by its passions and self-doubts, deluded by its own ideas, its distorted perceptions, its belief in an enduring personal identity, and its countless presuppositions and highly provisional explanations about the world and others. Such an undisciplined, chaotic mind will perpetually be in a state of suffering and turmoil and cause pain to all in its vicinity until it is quieted, then tamed by the meditation practices *(abhyasa)* outlined in the magnificent *Mahasatipatthana Sutra* (Great Mindfulness Discourse), where one learns to "abide contemplating feelings as feelings . . . mind as mind . . . [and] mind-objects as mind-objects."

There are, of course, numerous meditation traditions, but common to them all are exercises that provide a practitioner with but a single object for the mind's attention *(ekagrata)*. For beginners, the simplest exercise is offered by the body itself: one's own breath. Try, if you can, to observe for fifteen minutes *only* the rising-falling movement of your abdomen as you breathe. Soon enough, after a few seconds, as you attempt to focus on each inhalation and exhalation, you discover your mind drifting away from the breath—into memories, imaginings, daydreams, and perceptions of physical discomfort (an itch, a stiff back, and so on) as you try to sit perfectly still. (Another cartoonist, Frank Modell, captures this wonderfully when he asks, "It's ten o'clock. Do you know where your mind is?")

In Vipassana "insight meditation," for example, you do not ignore these fugitive wanderings of the mind, its tendency to go AWOL at the first opportunity, but instead carefully observe and identify each erumpent mental act as it appears, like clouds passing across the sky or waves on water—"reflecting," "planning," "feeling pain," "feeling pleasure," "feeling lazy," "feeling bored," "hearing a sound nearby"—and then you let them go, making no effort to hold on as you turn back to your breathing.

Over time this deceptively simple yet daunting exercise of just quietly tracking the labile mind's movements reveals, first, that each evanescent eruption of desire or emotion, each "imagining" or "feeling lazy," melts away like a mirage after it is vetted once or twice. Each is impermanent, with its own "arising and falling away" trajectory and, at bottom, is empty *(sunyata)*. Second, one realizes the unicity of what we call subject and object (the phenomenologist Edmund Husserl's terms were *noesis* and *noema*), which arise simultaneously in each flicker-flash instant of perception; they are ontologically twinned and inseparable, nondualistic, the one incapable of existing without the other. Put another way, the subject does not exist independent of an object, as David Hume noted two and a half centuries ago in his *Treatise of Human Nature*, where he pointed out, "For my part, when I enter most intimately into what I call *myself*, I always stumble on some particular perception or other, of heat or cold, light or shade, love or hatred, pain or pleasure, and can never observe anything but the perception."

From this elementary task of holding the mind to one's breathing, the beginner advances to attempting the same uninterrupted awareness not only when quietly sitting, but when engaged in other activities. The point of such concentration, which eventually flows seamlessly into meditation, is to attend with all one's heart and mind to the business at hand. Different schools of meditation employ a range of phenomenal "objects"—some physical, some mental—to achieve both that end and the spiritual goal of satori, or *moksha* (enlightenment). One might contemplate a symbolic image such as a mandala; a mental or physical picture of a beloved saint or savior, as practitioners of *bhakti* (devotion) prefer; or the visualizations characteristic of tantric yoga. Or one might repeat a single sound, or *mantra*, over and over, like the *Namu-myōhō-renge-kyō* of the Nichiren Buddhists.

* * *

Clearly, spiritual practice is nothing if it is not about attention. (The Sanskrit word for attention, *ekagrata,* can be translated as "one," *eka,* and "to seize," *grah.*) The same is true of reading and writing. Like a memory, a mathematical entity (numbers), or the visualizations in tantra, the aesthetic object experienced in any literary work is ontologically, as Jean-Paul Sartre points out in *What Is Literature?,* transcendent.

Open any novel. What is there? Black marks—signs—on white paper. First they are silent. They are lifeless, lacking signification until the consciousness of the reader imbues them with meaning, allowing a fictitious character like the nameless protagonist of Ralph Ellison's *Invisible Man,* say, to emerge powerfully from the monotonous rows of ebony type. This magical act is, of course, achieved through a concentration, as one reads, and an act of self-surrender that allows an entire fictional world to appear, redivivus, in the reader's mind: "a vivid and continuous dream," as the novelist John Gardner once called it. As readers, our focused awareness invests the cold signs on the pages of *Invisible Man* with *our* emotions, *our* understanding of oppression and fear. Then, in what is almost an act of thaumaturgy, the electrifying figures and situations Ellison has created reward us richly by returning our subjective feelings to us transformed, refined, and alchemized by language into a new vision with the capacity to change our lives forever.

That same *ekagrata* is at work on the writer's side of the creative equation, too, for the sustained and continuous fictional "dream" that the reader discovers was initially experienced by the author, who, to create an imaginary world, first had to visualize with vivid specificity each and every one of the thousands of details in his novel or short story.

For example, if a dramatic scene is richly evoked, placing us so thoroughly within its ambience that we forget the room we're sitting in or fail to hear the telephone ring; if in it we can "see" the *haecceitas* ("thisness") of every carefully described object on the fictional stage; if our senses imaginatively respond to, say, the quality of late-afternoon light as it falls upon the characters, and to imagery for evoking smells, sounds, and taste; if each revealing, moment-by-moment action, feeling, utterance, pause, and sigh of the characters is microscopically tracked and reverentially recorded by the writer, who, like an actor, must psychologically inhabit *all* the players at *every* moment in that scene; if every significant nuance of that scene is present with almost a palpable feel on the page, then it is because the radical attentiveness to detail, *here* and *now* in the mind's eye, demanded of the writer (who, knowing no division of creative labor, must in a single work of fiction play each principal role, be the set designer, director, costumer, hairstylist, makeup artist, lighting technician, prop master, casting director, dialogue and sound editor, location manager, and postproduction editor) is a species of the *ekagrata* (attention) practiced in meditation.

No story or novel I've been privileged to write came to me "whole." Rather, what I was initially given was a situation, dilemma, or character that intrigued me and caught my attention throughout the day, so that my curiosity compelled me to sit down to explore it further. What was—and always is—required for the seed of the story to flower was *greater* attention to all the prismatic possibilities of the imagined object, the story, plus the tossing aside of my own presuppositions concerning what the tale and its characters *should* be (I like to call this "beginner's mind"), until over time I've managed to strip away the interesting but inappropriate details and plot misdirections that do not lead to a complete, coherent, and consistent vision—never willing or forcing the fiction into existence, mind you, but instead scrupulously watching its manifestations from one draft to the next, then nurturing the moments that brought me the greatest sense of discovery. (My ratio of throwaway to keep pages is usually 20 to 1.) In other words, when I'm writing well, I am merely the servant of the story, its midwife.

And always this process, at least for me, involves letting go of the numerous ideas that arise during intense periods of creativity (ideas I might love and feel attached to) if they do not contribute to what John Barth once called a story's "ground situation"; and yes, like a *bhikshu* (Buddhist monk) dutifully counting his breaths or contemplating impermanence or compassion, I must repeatedly return my wandering mind again and again and yet again to the original spark for the tale: an especially demanding task for philosophical novels such as *Oxherding Tale, Middle Passage,* and *Dreamer,* which had five- and six-year gestation periods.

Yet for all its surface and subtle similarities to meditation, the sustained periods of *ekagrata* required for crafting finely wrought fiction do not in themselves lead to spiritual liberation. So much more is required for that. However, I'd like to believe that for a few literary artists, a lifetime spent harnessing the mind to the labor of creating transcendent objects can prepare them for the first, tentative steps on the Way. And I'm convinced, as I am of nothing else, that when mindfulness—so reverential toward all being—is brought to any task, irrespective of how humble, it transforms work into an opportunity to practice a form of worship that, as *The Dhammapada* puts it, "brings ease."

Accepting the Invitation

For a free people the franchise means everything. In a democratic republic, it is the proper name for empowerment. It is the essence of political equality. As the Reverend Joseph Carter put it in St. Francisville, Louisiana, in 1963, "A man is not a first-class citizen, a number one citizen, unless he is a voter."

But for nonwhite Americans and women, exercising this constitutional right involved a long, painful struggle from the nation's founding to the passage of the Voting Rights Act of 1965. This legislation, one of the primary goals of the Civil Rights movement, was achieved only after the agony of numerous campaigns sponsored by the National Association for the Advancement of Colored People, the Congress of Racial Equality, the Student Nonviolent Coordinating Committee, and the Southern Christian Leadership Conference to register eligible black voters throughout the South. Blacks who tried to vote were savagely beaten. Or hanged. They faced economic reprisals. Their homes were burned, their families driven out of town. Whites dropped snakes on those who stood in line to register. They obstructed black voters with preposterous "literacy tests" (when many illiterate whites were registered) and state poll taxes that were not outlawed in federal elections until the passage of the Twenty-fourth Amendment in 1964. American blacks paid for the precious franchise with their lives, among them Civil Rights workers James Chaney, Michael Schwerner, and Andrew Goodman, who were murdered for trying to register blacks in Alabama.

I've recited this grim, recent history because, as a Buddhist, I've long viewed the sphere of politics—and especially racial politics—to be the perfect illustration of *samsara*, or what the two-thousand-year-old sutra *The Perfection of Wisdom* calls *kamadhatu:* "the realm of desire," characterized by dualism and the hunger for power. It is a highly competitive world of Them vs. Us, of "winners" and "losers," where the Buddhist insight into "impermanence" is given concrete form as laws that may last only as long as the time between two elections. As one history teacher informed me when I was an undergraduate, one useful way to interpret any political document or piece of legislation is by first identifying in it the "screwer" and the "screwee," who always seem present in political affairs.

But for all my aversion to the polarizing dimensions of politics, I cannot forget Benjamin Franklin's haunting statement that "democracy is an invitation to struggle," which in the context of Dharma means struggle in the politicized realm of *samsara* that, paradoxically, is identical to *nirvana*—and doing so with the ironic understanding that, from an absolute standpoint, no one is struggling at all. And what does a Buddhist struggle for in the realm of relativity? The answer, I think, is twofold: to alleviate the suffering of all sentient beings and turn the Wheel of Dharma, as Thich Nhat Hanh and his monks did so beautifully during the Vietnam War, coming to the aid of orphans, widows, and the wounded on both sides of the civil war that devastated their country. Buddhism and politics need not be antithetical, as demonstrated by legendary King Ashoka, a lay follower of Buddhism who ruled the Maurya kingdom in northern India from 272–236 B.C.E., and in his edicts embraced generosity, compassion, refraining from killing, love of truth, inner insight, and harmonious relations with neighboring states.

One way to read the injunction for Right Conduct, an essential part of the Eightfold Path, is to see it as calling us—as citizens—to translate the Dharma into specific acts of social responsibility. In a democratic republic, that surely means voting for those initiatives that we believe will reduce suffering and violence, ignorance, and hatred—and the very divisions fueled by politics itself.

Thus, a Buddhist would not hesitate to vote for legislation and political candidates devoted to peace, to undoing injustice, reducing *duhka* in its myriad manifestations, healing society's wounds, preserving individual freedoms and the environment, as well as the rapidly vanishing forms of plant and animal life that are a part of it (and what Thich Nhat Hanh calls our "interbeing"). I do not feel that a Buddhist—whatever his or her tradition or lineage—must necessarily join a political party, for that often entails a blind allegiance that puts the party's survival and "winning" elections ahead of the ethical behavior outlined in the Eightfold Path. Rather, one can remain an "independent," supporting life-nurturing proposals and propositions wherever they arise, among Democrats or Republicans, the left or the right. (Once again, the samsaric language of a two-party political system plunges us into dualism!)

And yet, having just presented my arguments for why Buddhists should vote, I'm reminded of Dr. King's warning that only the spiritual life can lead to his goal of the "beloved community." "Racial justice . . . ," he wrote, "will come neither by our frail and often misguided efforts nor by God imposing his will on wayward men, but when enough people open their lives to God to allow Him to pour his triumphant, divine energy into their souls." In Buddhist terms, we must vote and use the means of the relative-phenomenal world to reduce suffering, for we are part of the relative-phenomenal world. But suffering will continue, despite our best efforts, until all of us experience—like Shakyamuni Buddha—enlightenment and liberation.

A Sangha by Another Name

The black experience in America, like the teachings of Shakyamuni Buddha, begins with suffering.

It begins in the violence of seventeenth-century slave forts sprinkled along the west coast of Africa, where debtors, thieves, war prisoners, and those who would not convert to Islam were separated from their families, branded, and sold to Europeans who packed them into pestilential ships that cargoed 20 million human beings (a conservative estimate) to the New World. Only 20 percent of those slaves survived the harrowing voyage at sea (and only 20 percent of the sailors, too), and if they were among the lucky few to set foot on American soil, new horrors and heartbreak awaited them.

As has been documented time and again, the life of a slave—our not-so-distant ancestors—was one of thinghood. It is, one might say, a frighteningly fertile ground for the growth of a deep appreciation for the First and Second Noble Truths as well as a living illustration of the meaning of impermanence. Former languages, religions, and cultures were erased, replaced by a Peculiar Institution in which the person of African descent was property, systematically—legally, physically, and culturally—denied all sense of self-worth. A slave owns nothing, least of all himself. He desires and dreams at the risk of his life, which is best described as relative to (white) others, a reaction to their deeds, judgments, and definitions of the world. And these definitions, applied to blacks, were not kind. In the nation's pulpits, Christian clergy in the South justified slavery by picturing blacks as the descendants of Ham or Cain; in his *Notes on the State of Virginia,* Thomas Jefferson dismissed slaves as childlike, stupid, and incapable of self-governance. For 244 years (from 1619 to 1863), America was a slave state with a guilty conscience: two and a half centuries tragically scarred by slave revolts, heroic black (and abolitionist) resistance to oppression, and, more than anything else, physical, spiritual, and psychological *suffering* so staggeringly thorough it silences the mind when we study the classic slave narratives of Olaudah Equiano or Frederick Douglass, or see the brutal legacies of chattel bondage in a PBS series like *Africans in America.* All that was over, of course, by the end of the Civil War, but the Emancipation Proclamation did not bring liberation.

Legal freedom instead brought segregation, America's version of apartheid, for another hundred years. But "separate" was clearly not "equal." The *experienced* law of black life was disenfranchisement, anger, racial dualism, second-class citizenship, and, as the great scholar W. E. B. Du Bois put it in his classic *The Souls of Black Folk* (1903), "double-consciousness." Can anyone doubt that if there is an essence—an *eidos*—to black American life, it has for three centuries been *craving,* and a quest for identity and liberty, which, pushed to its social extremes, propelled this pursuit beyond the relative, conceptual realities of race and culture to a deeper investigation of the meaning of freedom?

If the teachings of Shakyamuni Buddha are about *anything*, they are about a profound understanding of identity and the broadest possible meaning of liberty—teachings that sooner or later had to appeal to a people for whom suffering and loss were their daily bread. In the century after the Emancipation Proclamation, each generation of black Americans saw their lives disrupted by race riots, lynchings, and the destruction of entire towns and communities, such as the Greenwood district of black homes, businesses, and churches in Tulsa, Oklahoma, on May 31, 1921. These Jim Crow years witnessed the birth of the blues and a white backlash that fed poisonous caricatures of black people into popular culture and the national consciousness—films like *Birth of a Nation*, the writings of the Plantation School, and endless stereotypes that distorted black identity in newspapers and magazines—images that made the central questions of the black self "Who *am* I? American? African? Or something other? Can reality be found in any of these words?"

During these centuries of institutionalized denial, black Americans found in Christianity a spiritual rock and refuge. Although first imposed on some slaves by their owners as a way of making them obedient, Christianity in black hands became a means for revolt against bondage. Then, in the twentieth century, the black church provided consolation in a country divided by the color line. It became a common spiritual, social, economic, and political experience and was the place where black people could reinterpret Christianity and transform it into an instrument for worldly change. It became a racially tempered institution, one that raised funds to help the poor and to send black children off to college.

Historically, no other institution's influence compares with that of the black church, and I believe it will continue to be the dominant spiritual orientation of black Americans. It provides a compelling and time-tested moral vision, a metaphysically dualistic one that partitions the world into good and evil, heaven and hell; posits an immortal soul that no worldly suffering can harm; and through the agapic love of a merciful Father promises in the afterlife rewards denied in this one. Christianity, in part, made black Americans a genuinely Western people, on the whole identical in their strivings and sense of how the world works with Northern Europeans in the Judeo-Christian tradition.

But as early as 1923, Du Bois reflected deeply on the nature of black desires and a Western weltanschauung in a speech entitled "Criteria of Negro Art." It was published in *The Crisis*, the official publication of the National Association for the Advancement of Colored People, which Du Bois himself edited, and in this document he raises fundamental spiritual questions—what Buddhists might call Dharma doors—for a people whose dreams were long deferred.

What do we want? What is the thing we are after? As it was phrased last night it had a certain truth: We want to be Americans, full-fledged Americans, with all the rights of other American citizens. But is that all? Do we want simply to be Americans? Once in a while through all of us there flashes some clairvoyance, some clear idea, of what America really is. We who are dark can see America in a way that white Americans can not. And seeing our country thus, are we satisfied with its present goals and ideals?

If you tonight suddenly should become full-fledged Americans; if your color faded, or the color line here in Chicago was miraculously forgotten; suppose, too, you became at the same time rich and powerful;—what is it that you would want? What would you immediately seek? Would you buy the most powerful of motor-cars and outrace Cook County? Would you buy the most elaborate estate on the North Shore? Would you be a Rotarian or a Lion or a What-not of the very last degree? Would you wear the most striking clothes, give the richest dinners and buy the longest press notices?

Even as you visualize such ideals you know in your heart that these are not the things you really want. You realize this sooner than the average white American because, pushed aside as we have been in America, there has come to us not only a certain distaste for the tawdry and flamboyant but a vision of what the world could be if it were really a beautiful world; if we had the true spirit; if we had the Seeing Eye, the Cunning Hand, the Feeling Heart; if we had, to be sure, not perfect happiness, but plenty of good hard work, the inevitable suffering that always comes with life; sacrifice and waiting, all that—but, nevertheless, lived in a world where men know, where men create, where they realize themselves and where they enjoy life. It is that sort of a world we want to create for ourselves and for all America.

Others echoed Dr. Du Bois's question "What do we want?" As early as the 1920s, some black Americans were quietly investigating Far Eastern philosophies such as Hinduism and the Theravada and Mahayana traditions of Buddhism after experiencing Du Bois's "flashes of clairvoyance." Preeminent among these spiritual seekers was Jean Toomer, who regarded himself as "a psychological adventurer: one who, having had the stock experiences of mankind, sets out at right angles to all previous experience to discover new states of being." His classic work, *Cane* (1923), kicked off the Harlem Renaissance, the first outpouring of black American creativity after World War I. It is fitting, in a way, that *Cane*, a provocatively mystical work of fiction and poetry, inaugurated the Renaissance, which scholar Alain Locke described as the dawn of "The New Negro." Furthermore, the year after its publication, Toomer began the first of many summers in Europe studying, then teaching, the philosophy of Georges I. Gurdjieff, which remains an original restatement of esoteric wisdom influenced by Tibetan and Sufi teachings.

In 1931, Toomer self-published a remarkable collection of aphorisms entitled *Essentials*. Therein, he observed that "*I* is a word, but the worm is real," letting us know that the self was in part a product of language, which can conceal as much as it reveals about the world. He understood, as the earliest Buddhists did, that "the assumption of existence rests upon an uninterrupted series of pictures" and, more important, that "whatever is, is sacred." And he knew that all things were interdependent and transitory. He was no stranger to the renunciation of an illusory, empirical ego. Although his work after *Cane* was rejected by publishers, and he slipped into literary obscurity until the 1960s, Toomer was a spiritual trailblazer whose creative "journey to the east" inspired post-1960s authors, myself among them, to probe the "multiple simultaneous world" he first charted and to take to heart such aphorisms as "the realization of nothingness is the first act of being" and "we do not possess imagination enough to sense what we are missing."

If Toomer felt alone in his time ("It is as if I have seen," he said, "the end of things others pursue blindly"), he might have been comforted by the fact that some black American soldiers returning from service overseas came home with exposure to the Dharma—exposure that only increased as black soldiers brought back Korean and Japanese Buddhist wives. In his superb novel *Kingsblood Royal* (1947), Sinclair Lewis writes the story of a white man who discovers he has a black ancestor; he seeks to better understand people of color and realizes the great diversity of black Americans in his town—among them, writes Lewis, are Buddhists.

By the mid-1950s, as the Beats looked toward Zen, so did a few black musicians and poets; and of course by then the Civil Rights Movement was under way, led magnificently by Dr. Martin Luther King Jr., who took Mahatma Gandhi as his inspiration. After a pilgrimage to India in 1959, where he visited ashrams and sought to learn more about nonviolence not simply as a political strategy but as a way of life, King came back to America determined to set aside one day a week for meditation and fasting. In the 1960s, he nominated for the Nobel Peace Prize the outstanding Vietnamese Buddhist teacher Thich Nhat Hanh. King was, at bottom, a Baptist minister, yes, but one whose vision of the social gospel at its best complements the expansive, Mahayana *bodhisattva* ideal of laboring for the liberation of all sentient beings ("Strangely enough," he said, "I can never be what I ought to be until you are what you ought to be. You can never be what you ought to be until I am what I ought to be"). His dream of the "beloved community" is a Sangha by another name, for King believed, "It really boils down to this: that all of life is interrelated. We are caught in an inescapable network of mutuality, tied in a single garment of destiny."

The fourteen-year public ministry of Dr. King is emblematic of the philosophical changes that affected black Americans in the 1960s. Another milestone is the remarkable success of Soka Gakkai in attracting black Americans for three decades. Its members include entertainers with the high visibility of Herbie Hancock and Tina Turner. Although I do not belong to this Nichiren Buddhist group, which, according to writer Jane Hurst, represents 50,000 to 150,000 Americans (with 25–30 percent of these being black and Hispanic), my sister-in-law in Chicago and her friends are practitioners who have chanted *Namu-myōhō-renge-kyō* since the early 1970s.

In a recent conversation with my sister-in-law and one of her associates, I was informed that Soka Gakkai's initial attraction for them came about because they discovered that through chanting they could transform their lives and, in fact, that they alone were the architects of their own suffering and happiness. For my sister-in-law, raised Baptist and impoverished in a housing project on Chicago's South Side, the black church with its white Jesus had always been an unsatisfying experience, one from which she felt emotionally distant since childhood; for her friend, a woman raised as a Catholic, Soka Gakkai provided— through its explanation of karma and reincarnation and its foundation in the *Lotus Sutra*—a reason for the individual suffering she saw in the world, convincing her this was not due to the will of God but instead was based causally on each person's actions in this life and previous ones. Global peace is their goal. Chanting is their tool for self-transformation, empowerment, and experiencing the at-oneness with being they both had sought all their lives. *Namu-myōhō-renge-kyō*, they said, invested them with boundless energy, individual peace, and, as my sister-in-law's friend put it, "a natural high like I never had before."

Many white Buddhists new to the Zen and Tibetan traditions dismiss Soka Gakkai for what they consider its skewed, Christian-oriented, materialistic version of Buddhism. For me, Soka Gakkai is but one branch on the Bodhi tree. Yet its success in recruiting black Americans indicates that people of color find in

Buddhism the depths of their long-denied humanity; centuries-old methods of meditation—very empirical—for clearing the mind of socially manufactured illusions (as well as personally created ones); an ancient phenomenology of suffering, desire, and the self; and a path (the Eightfold Path) for a moral and civilized way of life.

The emphasis in Buddhist teachings on letting go of the fabricated, false sense of self positions issues of race as foremost among samsaric illusions, along with all the essentialist conceptions of difference that have caused so much human suffering and mischief since the eighteenth century. It frees one from dualistic models of epistemology that partition experience into separate, boxlike compartments of Mind and Body, Self and Other, Matter and Spirit—these divisions, one sees, are ontologically the correlates of racial divisions found in South African apartheid and American segregation and are just as pernicious.

More than anything else, the Dharma teaches mindfulness, the practice of being here and now in each present moment, without bringing yesterday's racial agonies into today or projecting oneself—one's hopes and longings—into a tomorrow that never comes. You watch the prismatic play of desires and emotions (for example: joy, fear, pride, and so-called black rage) as they arise in awareness, but without attachment or clinging to name and form, and then you let them go. One is especially free, on this path, from the belief in an enduring "personal identity," an "I" endlessly called upon to prove its worth and deny its inferiority in a world that so often mirrors back only negative images of the black self. Yet one need not cling to "positive" images either, for these, too, are essentially empty of meaning. Indeed, you recognize emptiness *(sunyata)* as the ultimate nature of reality. In my own fiction, I have worked to dramatize that insight in novels such as *Oxherding Tale* (1982), a slave narrative that serves as the vehicle for exploring Eastern philosophy; *Middle Passage* (1990), a sea adventure tale about the slave trade (and a rather Buddhist African tribe called the Allmuseri); and *Dreamer* (1998), a fictional account of the last two years of Martin Luther King's life that highlights his globally ecumenical spirituality.

Buddhist insights continue to multiply among contemporary black authors. In *Right Here, Right Now,* a recent novel by Trey Ellis, which won a 1999 American Book Award, we are offered the story of a black man who creates a new world religion that borrows heavily from Buddhism and underscores the central theme of impermanence and change. And Octavia Butler, a MacArthur fellow and much celebrated science-fiction writer, features in *Parable of the Sower* (1993) a narrator in 2024 who broods on the fact that "everyone knows that change is inevitable. From the second law of thermodynamics to Darwinian evolution, from Buddhism's insistence that nothing is permanent and all suffering results from our delusions of permanence to the third chapter of Ecclesiastes ('To every thing there is a season . . .'), change is part of life, of existence, of the common wisdom. But I don't believe we're dealing with all that that means. We haven't even begun to deal with it."

Canonical Zen documents like the "Ten Oxherding Pictures" of twelfth-century artist Kakuan Shien also appear in recent black poetry. In the preeminent journal of black letters, *Callaloo* (vol. 22, no. 1), the distinguished poet Lucille Clifton re-visioned the Ch'an teachings of the the "Ten Oxherding Pictures" in which the stages of Zen understanding are depicted by a man who follows the footsteps of an ox, which, untamed, represents ego. He finally glimpses the ox, slowly tames it, then trains it to do what he wants, not what ego wants. Only after he has completely transformed himself does he happily ride his ox back into the marketplace. Clifton writes these lines for the eighth picture, in which both the ox and oxherder disappear; here, the emptiness suggests the dissolution and arising of forms, and the essence of interdependence is represented by a circle:

The Ox and the Man Both Gone out of Sight

man is not ox
I am not ox
no thing is ox
all things are ox.

Through meditation, Du Bois's flashes of clairvoyance are sharpened and the internalized racial conflict of "double-consciousness" is transcended, enabling those of us who live in a violent, competitive society steeped in materialism to grasp the truth of impermanence *(anitya)* that first turned twenty-nine-year-old prince Siddhartha Gautama from the ephemeral sense pleasures of his palace to the pursuit of liberation and enlightenment. After he had abandoned experiencing the world through concepts and representations, after he realized the cessation of mental constructions, he perceived the interdependence of all things, how—as Thich Nhat Hanh says—"Everything is made of everything else, nothing can be by itself alone" *(anatman)* in a universe of ceaseless change and transformation. Then and only then is it possible to realize Dr. King's injunction that we "love our enemies" in the struggle for justice because once one approaches the "enemy" with love and compassion, the "enemy," the Other, is seen to be oneself.

All things, we learn, are ourselves. Thus, practice necessarily leads to empathy, the "Feeling Heart" Du Bois spoke of, Toomer's sense that all is sacred, and the experience of connectedness to all sentient beings. No matter how humble the activity—whether it be walking, sitting, eating, or washing the dishes—one approaches it with mindfulness, acting and listening egolessly as if this activity might be the most important thing in the world, for indeed all that is, has been, and will be is contained in the present moment. In this nondiscursive, expansive spirit, discrimination is inconceivable. After the practitioner has charged his battery, so to speak, in meditation, he eagerly works and creates to serve others—all others—with humility, a boundless joy in giving, fearlessness, and disinterest in all personal "rewards." And though the number of black Buddhists is small, they are growing in an increasingly multicultural America with the promise of more black people turning the Wheel of Dharma as a new millennium dawns. For through the Dharma, the black American quest for "freedom" realizes its profoundest, truest, and most revolutionary meaning.

On the Book of Proverbs

*W**here there is no vision, the people perish.*

Of all the practical observations in that most pragmatic of texts in the Old Testament, the Book of Proverbs, this one sentence linking vision and life comes singing off the page as the most profound. Meditate, please, on the possibility that in life there is a *goal*, an end that makes all our worldly efforts intelligible. Carefully think it through: without a *vision*, either personal or political, the individual (or society) is "like a city that is broken down, and without walls." This is not simply a question for the schools, for without a comprehensive and capacious philosophy life fails. The unsentimental implication here—the basic philosophical and secular premise—is that life can be a perilous journey. Perhaps a social minefield. (Just read today's newspaper if you need proof that the world is and has always been a dangerous place.) And any young person hesitantly starting out on this odyssey, now or in the days of King Solomon, soon discovers that his or her chances for survival, prosperity, and hap-

piness are enhanced a hundredfold if—and only if—he or she
has a good map.

Proverbs is that richly detailed, many-splendored map. A
timeless wake-up call. More important, along with its companion
books, the poetic "wisdom" literature of the Old Testament (Job,
Ecclesiastes, the Song of Solomon, and Psalms), it is a two-
millennia-old blueprint for the staggering challenge of living a
truly *civilized* life. Culture, we realize after reading Proverbs, is an
ongoing project. We are not born with culture. Or wisdom. And
both are but *one* generation deep. Achieving either is a daily task
requiring as much work for the individual as an artist puts into a
perfectly balanced painting, or a musician into a flawless performance. (Thus one wonders if the great bulk of humankind can
truthfully be called either cultured or civilized.) Here, in this
repository of moral instruction, in its 31 chapters, 915 verses,
approximately 900 proverbs, and 15,043 words, the journey that
we call a life is presented as a canvas upon which the individual
paints skillfully a civilized self-portrait—an offering—that will
please himself and the Lord. In chapter 3, we are told, "Happy is
the man that findeth wisdom." The Hebrew word for "wisdom"
is *chokmah*. It occurs no less than thirty-seven times in Proverbs.
Chokmah also means skillfulness in dealing with the job that is
before us—life itself—and I believe it is comparable to the Greek
word *techne*, the rational application of principles aimed at making or doing something well. The reader who takes Proverbs to
heart, who believes like the Greeks that "the unexamined life is
not worth living," is by nature a lover of wisdom: a philosopher.
For that is precisely what the word *philosophy* means (*philein*, "to
love"—*sophia*, "wisdom").

I'm aware those words—*wisdom, civilized,* and *philosophy*—
may sound musty and antique to modern (or postmodern) ears.
As so many have said, ours is an Era of Relativism, or situational

ethics, perhaps even of nihilism, a historical period in which Proverbs will for some readers seem right-wing and patriarchal, oppressive and harsh, dogmatic and illiberal. Many will regard its contents as obsolete for the conditions we face at the beginning of the twenty-first century because, above all else, we moderns value individual freedom. Unfortunately, our passion for liberty is often misunderstood as license or, more accurately, as licentiousness. Personally, as a Buddhist, I was at first wary of writing an essay about this book, though I was raised on its vision in a Midwestern, African Methodist Episcopal church. But after going over Proverbs a half dozen times, after opening myself to its spiritual core, which complements nicely the world's other great religious traditions, I rediscovered the gems it has offered Western humanity for centuries. I saw in its gnostic truths the reason why Professor C. E. M. Joad once defined decadence as "the loss of an object in life." I realized that Proverbs not only speaks powerfully to our morally adrift era, but describes rather well my own often benighted, rebellious-on-principle generation (the baby boomers) when it says, "There is a generation that curseth their father, and doth not bless their mother. There is a generation that are pure in their own eyes, and yet is not washed from their filthiness" (30:11–12).

Chilling.

Like all rich, multilayered digests, Proverbs was not the work of a day. Nor is it the product of a single author, though King Solomon, that ur-figure among ancient wise men, is credited with having contributed two of its oldest sections (1:1 and 1:10). Several centuries after the death of Israel's king, the men of Hezekiah (700 B.C.E.) added chapters 25 through 29 from Solomonic material. The book was built layer upon layer, one tissue at a time, borrowing its synthesized instructions from many ancient sources, and did not achieve its finished form until the fourth or fifth century B.C.E.. It favors, one might say, an old, old coin that has traversed continents, picking up something from each one as it was passed down through centuries—advice on social etiquette, philanthropy, how to choose a wife, and why children may need an occasional dose of Dr. Spanker's tonic (the "rod")—and bears the sweat and palm oil of millions who have handled it. Bible scholar Kenneth T. Aitken persuasively argues in his commentary *Proverbs* that the third section of the text (chapter 22) takes a few pages from the *Instructions of Amenemopet.*[1] That work, dating back to between 1000 and 600 B.C.E., was strictly a manual of professional training aimed at helping Egyptian civil servants achieve successful careers as they served the state. The sages of Israel, says Aitken, reworked some of the precepts from *Instructions* and at the same time recontextualized them in a book far broader in its teachings for a triumphant life.

And these were, of course, originally *oral* teachings. They were delivered by a sage to pupils he addressed as a father would his children. His young charges were expected to memorize the proverbs until they were hard-wired into their hearts. This book was written for the ear. It relies heavily on repetition, a mnemonic device (which might weary modern eyes), and in its compositional strategies employs couplets linked by parallelisms. In his exegesis of Proverbs, J. Vernon McGee identifies three forms of parallelisms that occur in the text: (1) *Synonymous Parallelism*, where the second clause restates the content of the first ("Judgments are prepared for scorners, and stripes for the back of the fool," 19:29); (2) *Antithetic (Contrast) Parallelism*, which states a truth in the first clause, then contrasts it with an opposite truth in the second ("The light of the righteous rejoiceth, but the lamp of the wicked shall be put out," 13:9); and (3) *Synthetic Parallelism*, in which the second clause devel-

CHARLES JOHNSON

ops the truth of the first ("The terror of a king is as the roaring of a lion; whoso provoketh him to anger sinneth against his own life," 20:2).[2]

Yet for all the sophisticated architectonics in Proverbs, and for all the complexity of its literary pedigree, this is a book that sketches out a compelling, classic story: a pilgrim's progress. Imagine a young man (or woman) about to embark on life's journey. Call him—well, Pilgrim. Then, as now, the world teemed with a kaleidoscope of temptations, stramash, and confusion. In the bustling cities where colorful bazaars, beggers, thieves, perfumed harlots, con men, murderers, insouciant idlers, and false teachers eager to entice a young person toward wrongdoing and sin (one hoary meaning of which is "to miss the mark"), all can be found in great abundance. These players, some as beautiful as Satan and who say, "Let us lie in wait for blood, let us lurk privily for the innocent," have from time immemorial taken advantage of callow youths (as well as given writers as diverse as Voltaire, de Sade, Dickens, Fielding, and Maugham inexhaustible material for the bildungsroman). Given a strictly materialistic viewpoint, it follows that the world of matter, mere *stuff,* will be dominated everywhere and in any era by those who treat objects and others as *things* to be used for their own pleasure and profit, and view everything through the lens of their own limited consciousness. Surveying this social field, we can imagine the authors of Proverbs agreeing with Thomas à Kempis, who, in *The Imitation of Christ,* wearily quotes the Stoic philosopher Seneca, "A wise man once said, 'As often as I have been among men, I have returned home a lesser man' . . . No man can live in the public eye without risk to his soul."[3]

As we have seen, if our young Pilgrim is not to lose his (or her) soul on this planet where everything is provisional, if he is not to end bellied up and bottomed out, he needs a damned good map. Ethically, he should not have to reinvent the wheel each time he is confronted by a new moral dilemma. That, I believe, would be like a physicist claiming he can learn nothing from Galileo, Newton, Copernicus, or Einstein because the conditions of their time differed so much from his own. But young people are notorious for forgetting instructions (ask any teacher about that), especially the nine hundred lessons on living delivered in Proverbs. What Pilgrim needs is the teaching condensed into *one* simple, bare-knuckled mantra that encapsulates the pith of all the other proverbs. Anticipating just this problem, the Proverbs authors provide that axiom in the very first chapter: "The fear of the Lord is the beginning of knowledge: but fools despise wisdom and instruction." From this one antithetic parallelism, this stern and admonishing couplet—moment-by-moment mindfulness of the Most High—all else in Proverbs follows with mandarin exactitude and the necessity of a logical proof. Pilgrim is counseled to "Commit thy works unto the Lord, and thy thoughts shall be established" (16:3), for the authors of this text understood the irrefragable fact that all we are is the result of what we have thought. From intellection comes desire. From desire, will. From will, our deeds. And from deeds, our destiny. Self-control, therefore, is so essential for the spiritual life and a practical life well led that it is even favorably compared to martial conquest—"He that is slow to anger is better than the mighty; and he that ruleth his spirit than he that taketh a city" (16:32)—in a line strikingly similar to one equally famous that we find in the first-century B.C.E. Buddhist *Dhammapada* ("Path of Virtue")—"If one man conquer in battle a thousand times a thousand men, and if another conquers himself, he is the greatest of conquerors."[4] In the world's religious traditions, Eastern and Western, the Way of understanding and wisdom begins by sumptuously feeding the spirit and starving the illusory sense of the ego into extinction ("Trust in the Lord with all thine heart; and lean not unto thine own understanding. In all thy ways acknowledge him, and he shall direct thy paths. Be not wise in thine own eyes" [3:5–7]) and is realized through a worldly practice that gives priority to the experience of our elders (our global inheritance) over ephemera in a life that embodies humility, service, and a culture's loftiest ideals, which in Pilgrim's case would be the Ten Commandments.

Wisdom in Proverbs, we might say, is thought winging its way home.

Naturally, many couplets in Proverbs inveigh against people who are *not* mindful, those who "eat the bread of wickedness and drink the wine of violence," and break the Commandments. This book does not suffer fools gladly. At first glance, Pilgrim might see the less demanding, hedonistic path and its players as alluring and sweet—and fun! But the seeds of Proverbs (practical wisdom) cannot grow in that polluted soil (the "froward"). Pilgrim is advised not to envy or even "fret" over the fallen state of these caitiffs and poltroons, for the Lord shall "render to every man according to his works." In other words, just as there is inexorable causation in the physical realm, so, too, is there cause and effect in the moral universe. The kingdom of God, at bottom, is a meritocracy; its logic is that of *karma* ("as you sow so shall you reap"). The unmindful cause their own downfall— they "eat of the fruit of their own way." Time and again, Proverbs drives this point home, and nowhere more vividly than in its parable-like description of the industrious ant, or when the book cautions against lapses of vigilance in language so lovely the words almost pirouette and leap on the page: "Yet a little sleep, a little slumber, a little folding of the hands to sleep: so shall thy poverty come as one that traveleth; and thy want as an armed man" (24:33–34).

However, it would be wrong to say that Proverbs is simply a map for avoiding life's pitfalls in order to bow one's knees to Baal. Throughout its chapters, Pilgrim is urged, "Labor not to be rich," and he is reminded how "riches certainly make themselves wings; they fly away as an eagle toward heaven," and "better is the poor that walketh in his uprightness, than he that is perverse in his ways, though he be rich." Does this advice contradict the practicality that infuses Proverbs? Does it ask us to be poor? No, for a crucial distinction is drawn: "Wealth gotten by vanity shall be diminished: but he that gathereth by labor shall increase." The book points our Pilgrim toward industry, not that he might be "greedy of gain," but rather that he or she might become the sort of provider who "leaveth an inheritance to his children's children," honors his mother and father (and, one might add, his teachers), and "stretcheth out her hand to the poor." In effect, Pilgrim's labor is for others. Always life's true wealth in Proverbs is found in God, in wisdom and love; and love is realized through work and indefatigable service to the things loved.

In Proverbs, the portrait—the character sketch—that emerges of a successful pilgrim is that of a man or woman who is a quiet embodiment of culture. Not perfect by any means because he knows all too well his flaws. But in his life of building, serving, creating, he mightily strives to be righteous. He is soft-spoken and hates lying. In him there is the continuity of generations, one of the requisites for civilization itself. He is the joy of his mother and father and his children as well, for by honoring the wisdom of his predecessors and transmitting that (along with the fruit of his industry) to his posterity, his past (parents) meets his present (children) and vouchsafes their future. His good name the pilgrim values highly, and he is not garrulous, knowing how to hold his tongue and keep his own counsel. He never acts rashly or "answereth a matter before he heareth it." Concerning the needy, he is socially conscious and never "stoppeth his ears at the cry of the poor." Though he experiences failure and "falleth seven times," the just man struggles to his feet again to do the Lord's work, ignoring his weariness. According to Proverbs, at night his sleep is "sweet." Such a person always heeds the helpful criticism of friends, but never wearies them with his presence or overstays his welcome. And, despite his hard-won victories and integrity, he never boasts, allowing instead "another man [to] praise thee, and not thine own mouth." Finally, the man of mindfulness is the very foundation of society—"bold as a lion," the sort of citizen who, if he assumes a position of authority in the state, makes the "people rejoice."

Clearly, the path mapped out in Proverbs is exacting. Straight and narrow, "like the edge of a sword," as Mahatma Gandhi once described the spiritual life. It is fitting, then, that Proverbs ends by letting our pilgrim know that he need not—indeed *cannot*—travel to his goal alone. The righteous man needs a companion, a spouse equally mindful and just who will "do him good and not evil all the days of her life." A life partner of such luminous morality that his heart "doth safely trust in her, so that he shall have no need of spoil." And so, in its remarkable finale—just before the curtain falls—this Old Testament book extolling wisdom and virtue closes by incarnating its heady idealism in an astonishing homage to the *concrete* beauty and goodness of God-fearing women (one surely influential for Chaucer's Wife of Bath), a breathtaking, unforgettable praise-song to this "good thing," this "favor of the Lord," this ravishing "wife of thy youth":

> *Strength and honor are her clothing;*
> *and she shall rejoice in time to come.*

She openeth her mouth with wisdom;
and in her tongue is the law of kindness.
She looketh well to the ways of her household,
and eateth not the bread of idleness.
Her children arise up and call her blessed;
her husband also, and he praiseth her.

May we all be blessed with such radiant partners. And as we travel through this life, may we recognize that Proverbs, in its fierce, uncompromising purity, is a work worthy of our trust.

A Poet of Being

We do not possess imagination enough to sense what we are missing.

—*Jean Toomer*

Can a black writer be too profound, too visionary, and too expansive for a general American readership?

I would wager that this question about authors and audiences nagged poet-philosopher Jean Toomer his entire life. In American literary history he is unique. A metaphysical seeker and searcher. A pioneering genius, which is a polite way of saying that among black writers (and most white ones) in the first half of the twentieth century he is a glorious oddity. To put it bluntly, colored men were not supposed to think about the perennial epistemological and ontological questions—Western and Eastern—that absorbed Toomer, or to think about them so damned well. Not then nor today are these widely considered proper subjects for black men. Personally, I cannot believe at the time Toomer wrote his finest work that either whites—conservative, liberal, or radical—or most Negroes were prepared for a black poet of Being who believed that "the true critic is a critic of meaning and of values."

During one of the most entrenched periods of apartheid in the United States—the 1920s and 1930s—Toomer stated, "I am of no particular race. I am of the human race, a man at large in the human world, preparing a new race." (A new what? More on this remarkable claim in a moment.) In the Roaring Twenties, with its bathtub gin, pleasure-seeking jazz-babies, Marcus Garvey's "Back to Africa" movement, and a postwar materialism and scientism that alarmed both phenomenologist Edmund Husserl and humanist Albert Schweitzer, Toomer—a writer as inwardly oriented as Herman Hesse—takes the spiritual temperature of his era and discovers that "failing to achieve intangible satisfactions, we are compelled to accept tangible dissatisfactions." During a Great Depression that fueled European fascism, the rise of racial eugenics, and black lynchings throughout the South, this man only three generations removed from slavery dared to portray himself as "a psychological adventurer: one who, having had the stock experiences of mankind, sets out at right angles to all previous experience to discover new states of being."

The underpublished author of *Essentials*, who strove to be "not conformative but formative," must often have felt painfully misunderstood, ahead of—and out of step with—the literary and racial worlds. "It is as if I have seen the end of things others pursue blindly," Toomer wrote. His spirit had a Hegelian restlessness. According to scholar Rudolph Byrd, after repeated rejection from publishers, Toomer started Lakeside Press, the mission of which was "to encourage, secure, publish, and distribute quality literature dealing with all phases of spiritual experience. . . . Most of the first-rate publishers have no particular interest in such material and, if submitted to them, they are likely to reject it. This is because their tastes and values have been conditioned by nineteenth-century naturalism and rationalism, or by materialism."

Ironically, those same publishers had praised Toomer earlier for *Cane,* a hypnotic, language-rich montage of poetry and short fiction that delivers a portrait of Southern black life so mythic and shot through with elemental mysteries that it clearly belongs in the tradition of American transcendentalism stretching back to Emerson and Thoreau. Indeed, *Cane* is regarded as the inaugural work of the Harlem Renaissance. But for Toomer, again ironically, the publishers who urged him to repeat himself with a replay of *Cane* might well have misread his classic because, as Toomer put it, their interest in Negro art in the 1920s was primarily for "'back to nature and the primitive,' exotic, or erotic leanings." In our time a corollary would be the opinion of the reading public and publishers that the most authentic black writing is "political," or about racism, or about the social pathologies of the inner city, as if the portrayal of black life can only truly be convincing if it concerns some form of reaction to white oppression.

Far too many critics of Toomer give only a glancingly brief examination to his ideas, usually implying that his thought was derivative and unoriginal, gleaned primarily from Georges I. Gurdjieff who, as Richard K. Barksdale and Keneth Kinnamon put it in *Black Writers of America,* "combined elements of Yoga, religious mysticism, and Freud into a system he called Unitism." As *Essentials* shows, this assessment does Toomer— and us—a great disservice, and it does not acknowledge well enough Gurdjieff's own indebtedness to Buddhism and Hinduism. While he may have been a disciple of Gurdjieff, and even have eagerly taught at his institute, Toomer's creative work in the

1930s in two forms—the aphorism and poetry like "Blue Meridian"—reveals a first-rate, elegant mind attempting to transcend false concepts of Western dualism and to ontologically restore to our sense of life its original wholeness, as well as the universe's enduring mystery, which human arrogance always denies. Toomer aphorizes: "Science is a system of exact mysteries" and "We who talk of knowledge cannot sense the nature of an apple." He also has a delicious knack for wit and irony.

I recommend that readers experience *Essentials* and "Blue Meridian" (1937) at the same time. In the latter, a sweeping Whitmanesque song of this country's possibilities that also offers us a bridge between the black experience and the profound reflections on selfhood long a part of Vedic literature, Toomer prophesies that the new man of tomorrow's America will be a "blue man." In my reading of this poem, he selects this color to invoke the image of Krishna in Hindu pictorial art, in which that deity's skin is as blue and borderless as the sky itself, thereby suggesting the infinity and nonduality of being.

Toomer's "new (blue) man" is therefore emblematic of a being as enlightened and liberated as any *bodhissatva*, beyond likes and dislikes, "prejudices and preferences." He is a cross-cultural being, a breaker of polarities. Thus when Toomer writes, "It is a new America / To be spiritualized by each new America," he urges us to avoid all forms of bondage and enslavement, from without and especially from within. Toomer urges:

> *Let go!*
> *Let it go that we may live.*
> *A pin, a watch-fob, a card of identification,*
> *A name, pain and emptiness,*
> *A will to perpetuate what has been, blind*

To distinctions between the useful and the
  Useless,
And, of course, an ego.
Let go!
That which you have held has got hold of you
And would sink you as it goes down.

He understood, as all spiritual seekers do, that our true enslavement and freedom begins first in the mind, in a consciousness that a racially fractured society, vulgar materialism, and naive naturalism have corrupted. Toomer continues:

Uncase the races,
Open this pod,
Free man from this shrinkage,
Not from the reality itself,
But from the unbecoming and enslaving behavior
Associated with our prejudices and preferences.
Eliminate these;
I am, we are, simply of the human race . . .
Free the sexes,
I am neither male nor female or in-between;
I am of sex, with male differentiations . . .
Expand the fields—
Those definitions which fix fractions
  and lose wholes—
I am of the field of being,
We are beings.

Compare those lines to the opening of the *Dhammapada,* a first-century B.C.E. Buddhist classic text: "All that we are is the result of what we have thought." From thought comes desire. From desire, will. From will, our deeds. And from deeds, our destiny. In his quest for meaning, Toomer seems to have arrived at his own important Dharma principles such as the interdependence of all things and their transitoriness. In "Blue Meridian," he writes:

> *And we are the old people; we are witnesses*
> *That behind us there extends*
> *An unbroken chain of ancestors, linking us*
> *To all who ever lived and will live.*

(What a shame this poem was not selected by Presidents Kennedy and Clinton to be read at their inaugurals.)

Published six years before "Blue Meridian," *Essentials* probes these questions in a form—the aphorism—made philosophically viable by thinkers of the caliber of Friedrich Nietzsche in *Beyond Good and Evil*. Can we speak of the general topography of Toomer's thought in this luminous, little volume? Of how *Essentials* portrays Man and World? I believe we can, but only if we acknowledge his dialectical approach for describing phenomenon, a style of thinking exemplified by his statement that "the realization of nothingness is the first act of being." This at first brings to mind Sartrean existentialism, though it would be a mistake to let our examination of this proposition rest there. No, a more fruitful tack would be to go beyond—and far behind—Sartre to early Buddhist thought, reading the Void, or *sunyata*, for "nothingness." By such a move we establish—as I think Toomer would wish us to do—"nothingness" as a fullness, a plenum of undifferentiated being, rather than as a vacuity or emptiness, and "being" as that fullness's momentary and ephemeral manifestation.

In one very telling line, he writes, "*I* is a word, but the worm is real," and follows that with the apothegm "Unless a man dies consciously he will die," meaning (as in the famous poem by St. Francis, the last line of which is "It is in dying that we are born to eternal life") that the "I" is a delusion created by the limitations of language. Toomer wrote, "In this multiple simultaneous world words only dole out one thing at a time." "I" is a chimera, a point David Hume's radically empirical methodology made clear two and a half centuries ago in *A Treatise of Human Nature* in which he wrote, "For my part, when I enter most intimately into what I call *myself*, I always stumble on some particular perception or other, of heat or cold, light or shade, love or hatred, pain or pleasure. I can never catch myself at any time without a perception, and never can observe anything but the perception." Toomer's critique of the self in *Essentials*— "The assumption of existence rests upon an uninterrupted and unchallenged series of pictures"—compares favorably with very ancient wisdom found in the second- or third-century Vedanta text the *Astavakra Samhita*, chapter 8, verse 4:

यदा नाहं तदा मोक्षो यदाहं बन्धनं तदा

Where there is no I, there is liberation;
when there is I, there is bondage

Toomer's belief that what we call the self (the subjective side of experience) is without substance—is not an *essence*—leads seamlessly to Toomer's assessment of the "objective" world, to his awareness of how nuclear physics in the 1920s was revealing "matter" to be no more than a concept or abstraction, for beneath the visible world of the senses, which most people believe is substantive, there is a dynamic, invisible reality of protons, electrons, and hadrons in constant movement, transformation, and mutation. "While the world produced by science, the technical, industrial world, is growing more materialistic," he wrote, "science itself is growing more immaterial." If that be the case, if theoretical subatomic physics was dissolving the perceived world of mere *stuff* before our eyes; if Sir James Jeans was correct in saying that the real structure of reality is more like a great thought than a machine driven by matter and if Sir Arthur Eddington did not err in remarking that "the external world of physics has become a world of shadows. In removing our illusions we remove substance, for indeed we have seen that substance is one of the greatest of our illusions"; if all of this is credible, then Toomer can say—and does dare to say—that "the existence of the body, like the existence of the soul, is a matter of belief." This observation would no doubt please metaphysician Joel S. Goldsmith, who, in *Living Between Two Worlds*, wrote, "The mystery is not how a material world came about, but rather the discovery that it never did."

From the first of *Essentials*'s aphorisms to the last we find one underlying message expressed again and again: "whatever is, is sacred." That conviction, that reverence for all life, made Toomer, at his core, a religious artist—"Religion is that which relates one to oneself and to all other existences," he wrote— who during his intellectual odyssey glimpsed that no writer can produce great, lasting literature from a fragmented, unexamined life. He continues: "One must become a man before he can be an artist." It also made him one of the most valuable—and moral—black poet-philosophers of the twentieth century, an artist whose "psychological adventures" paved the way for many writers who followed in the 1960s and 1970s, when black naturalistic fiction began to be replaced by stories and novels that sought to capture the "multiple simultaneous world" that Toomer had first attempted to chart. For me, he is a spiritual brother; a fellow traveler; a co-member of the Buddhist community or Sangha. A seeker who heroically cleared a path on which I was blessed to find such works as *Oxherding Tale, Middle Passage,* and *Dreamer.*

For American literature in this century and the next, Toomer is indeed essential.

Toro Nagashi

Every year on August 6 and also August 9, people who love peace here in America, in Japan, and other parts of the world participate in the Lantern Floating Ceremony. It was my pleasure to do so in 2001 in Seattle. Our desire was to remember not only those who died in 1945 at Hiroshima and Nagasaki, but also all the victims of violence worldwide. "From Hiroshima to Hope" is an event based on an ancient Buddhist ritual, Toro Nagashi. But it is not a ceremony for Buddhists alone. And in Seattle, two years ago, it had special significance. In the winter of 2001, during the Mardi Gras festivities in Pioneer Square, one young man, Kristopher Kime, lost his life to violence, and seventy-one people were injured. On May 31, a black man named Aaron Roberts was killed in the Central District by a police officer. His death, the second killing of a black male by Seattle police since this century began, triggered months of racial tension that resulted on July 7 in an assault on Mayor Paul Schell at an event that community organizers hoped would create greater unity.

I am a Buddhist. And if I understand Toro Nagashi at all, I saw this beautiful ceremony, which brought us all together, as the occasion for two things. First, we floated candlelit paper lanterns on Green Lake to remember and mourn all the lives lost because of violence in its many forms. And, secondly, this event demanded that each and every one of us reflect deeply on the causes of violence and how we can remove them from our own lives. This is *not* an easy task. It has *never* been easy because we live in a culture where different forms of violence have become recreation and entertainment. Our popular films and fiction are violent. On our highways we have "road rage." Domestic violence against women continues, and we have not seen the end of hate crimes against people of color and citizens who are gay. Ethnic and religious violence erupt almost every day in the Middle East, England, Afghanistan, Africa, and from coast to coast in America, where some people see the emotion of "anger" as being righteous and justified.

I believe this ceremony helped us to understand that *all* forms of violence—which arise from anger, hatred, and fear—are *un*acceptable for a civilized people. Toro Nagashi asks us to imagine the unimaginable: What would it be like if we could somehow live a nonviolent life twenty-four hours a day, seven days a week. Violence is not only physical. It is also psychological and verbal. Violence can exist in our spirits. Violence can appear wherever and whenever our own *egos* lead us to believe that we and our destinies are separate from others. Violence appears when we speak harshly to or about others. In other words, violence first begins in the *mind* when we think dualistically, and when we forget that *every*one on earth simply wants the same two things that we want—happiness and to avoid suffering.

There is a very old Buddhist idea that I believe this ceremony represented. It is known as the Four Right Procedures.

The first right procedure is to prevent evil or violence from starting. The second is to remove any evil or violence as soon as it starts. The third is to encourage acts of peace and nonviolence. And the fourth is to nurture the growth and continuance of actions that lead to goodwill and the recognition that all our lives are interrelated.

That night, two years ago, my hope for those of us in Seattle, and around the world, was that we might carry the spirit of this ceremony into every dimension of our daily lives. I hoped also that we would remember the statement of one of our greatest civil rights leaders, Dr. Martin Luther King Jr. What he said applies to all of us as parents and children, as teachers and students, as husbands and wives, as citizens and neighbors. "We are all caught in an inescapable network of mutuality, tied in a single garment of destiny. Whatever affects one directly, affects all indirectly."

On
Writing

The Role of the Black Intellectual
in the Twenty-first Century

Anyone interested in the direction black intellectuals should take in the dawning twenty-first century need look no further for clues than the Modern Library's "100 Best Nonfiction Books of the 20th Century." In a way, this somewhat controversial brief on "the best that has been known and said in the world" (to borrow a phrase from Matthew Arnold) in English during the last one hundred years encapsulates the essential dilemma of the black scholar working within a predominantly white society at century's end. The list was voted on by a panel of thirteen authors that included A. S. Byatt, Caleb Carr, Christopher Cerf, Shelby Foote, Stephen Jay Gould, Vartan Gregorian, John Krakauer, Edmund Morris, Elaine Pagels, John Richardson, Arthur Schlesinger Jr., Carolyn See, and myself.

The Modern Library list is, of course, not the only compilation of "the best." At the eleventh hour of the twentieth century it was difficult to resist the temptation to make new catalogs for almost every field and discipline. Thus, we also had *Sacred Fire: The QBR 100 Essential Black Books,* edited by Max Rodriquez, founder of *Quarterly Black Review of Books,* which contains my foreword; as well as the Modern Library's "100 Best English-Language Novels," which contains only three black works of fiction (*Native Son, Invisible Man,* and *Go Tell It on the Mountain*); and the American Film Institute's "100 Top American Films," a much-publicized list that included not a single motion picture written, directed, or produced by persons of color.

Of all these lists the Modern Library's nonfiction catalog is the most instructive for black intellectuals. Out of one hundred books only seven are by African-Americans. These are *Up from Slavery* by Booker T. Washington, *Black Boy* by Richard Wright, *Notes of a Native Son* by James Baldwin, *The Souls of Black Folk* by W. E. B. Du Bois, *The Autobiography of Malcolm X* by Alex Haley and Malcolm X, *Why We Can't Wait* by Martin Luther King Jr., and *Shadow and Act* by Ralph Ellison. To be sure, these texts are among the most influential, discussed, and debated books in black literature since 1901. No one can doubt that they have been foundational—indeed *seminal*—for any and all discussions of race for the last five generations.

But compare now these "black" titles to the ones by white authors on the Modern Library listing. William James explores *The Varieties of Religious Experience;* John Maynard Keynes offers *The General Theory of Employment, Interest and Money;* G. E. Moore gives us *Principia Ethica;* and Lewis Thomas explores *The Lives of a Cell.* Readers would have to be blind not to see that the intellectual commerce represented by white authors ranges over all possible subjects and phenomena—from mathematics (*Principia Mathematica*) to literary criticism (*Aspects of the Novel*), history (*The Making of the Atomic Bomb*) to philosophy (*A Theory of Justice*)—including titles on race (*An American Dilemma* and *The Strange Career of Jim Crow*) while the work of black intellectuals is confined to race alone.

The *QBR 100 Essential Black Books* only reinforces this depressing revelation since it consists entirely of works devoted to some dimension of the race problem. We must ask: How can it be that African-American intellectuals have not produced watershed *non*racial works in the last one hundred years?

If I'm not mistaken, the answer can be found in the peculiar, limiting role assigned to black "intellectuals" in the twentieth century. From Booker T. Washington to Wright and Ellison and Baldwin, from Amiri Baraka to Toni Morrison, Henry Louis Gates Jr. and Cornel West, the *role* of the black "intellectual" has been, first and foremost, that of (1) interpreting as a spokesperson the "black experience" to white people during the Jim Crow and post–Civil Rights periods, and (2) addressing his or her literary and intellectual efforts *not* to the mysterious, inexhaustible world at large, *not* to the vast universe of unvoiced subjects that await exploration, but instead to that smaller province of meaning assigned to people of color. To put this bluntly, twentieth-century black "intellectuals" were granted authority by the white world on but one worldly subject: *themselves.*

How could it be otherwise? Since the 1960s whites dare not speak on black subjects, regardless of how much research they may have done, because they lack "the authority of experience" that comes from being born and raised black. Thus, our "intellectuals" have the field of race all to themselves in what looks dangerously to be the *re*segregation of the black mind. Needless to say, this territorial claim has been profitable in the short term for many black American writers, leading to six-figure book contracts (always on racial subjects), prestigious awards, much publicity in the media, high-profile status on the nation's talk shows, and very comfortable careers. The black "public intellectual," as he or she has been recently called, enjoys in America a celebrity hitherto unknown to predecesors like sociologist E. Franklin Frazier and Charles S. Johnson. He is called upon to comment, on television or radio or in the newspapers, on every new wrinkle in black life, whether that be the controversy over Ebonics, the death of Tupac Shakur, the O. J. Simpson trial, a recent comment by Nation of Islam leader Louis Farrakhan, the "black take" on President Clinton's affair with Monica Lewinsky, or some other event in the African Diaspora, though clearly his opinions outside his field of specialization carry no more weight than those of the proverbial man on the street—and seldom (if ever) is he asked to speak with professional authority on scientific, technological, religious, or nonracial international affairs that affect the state of the republic. *Those* are still the province of white and, lately, Asian scholars.

As you may have noticed I've been placing sneer quotes around the word *intellectual.* This is not to denigrate our cultural workers today but to indicate that it is important to distinguish between *scholars* and *intellectuals.* When asked to define the latter, Bertrand Russell once replied, "I have never called myself an intellectual, and nobody has ever dared to call me one in my presence. . . . I think an intellectual may be defined as a person who pretends to have more intellect than he has, and I hope that definition does not fit me." Before the twentieth century the term *intellectual* most often carried a negative meaning, denoting someone who reduced all knowing to pure reason. According to historian Russell Kirk, such "intellectuals" were denounced as sophists who overrated the intellect by *scholars* as various as Bacon, Hume, and Coleridge. The true scholar, we come to see, is a man or woman of genuine epistemological humility, someone who realizes that what we know, as Russell pointed out, is always "vanishingly small." Today, however, the black "intellectual" is all too often an informed pundit who presents his judgments and opinions in a public, mass market forum, rather than to colleagues, and the result is often comic when the "intellectual-celebrity" steps out of the field where he or she has genuine authority (artists, for example, who talk about the fields of economics or politics when they are amateurs; or, if you like, Morrison's recent statement that William Jefferson Clinton is our first "black" president, which was probably news to everyone in Clinton's family).

Celebrity, in short, can be as poisonous for contemporary intellectual integrity as the centuries-old ghettoizing of the black intellect and imagination. When one's reputation is founded not so much on a groundbreaking work of scholarship but rather on being well-known, it follows that one must strive mightily to stay newsworthy, no matter how shallow, hastily executed, or ephemeral one's work becomes. The painstaking, slow work of scholarship becomes replaced by media appearances, often shameless self-promotion, and even the dubious distinction of being "controversial" buys one a headline in the press and Andy Warhol's fifteen minutes of fame on the Oprah Winfrey show. But consider the reaction of Jean Genet when a reporter asked him how he felt about his becoming famous so fast. Genet replied that he wanted not fame but glory—and *that* only came long after a writer was dead. In other words, we can only see an author's work having critical significance in intellectual history if it endures for at least fifty years, finding its audience among several generations, each of which discovers in his text something of value for their own time as well as an enduring disclosure of the subject the author had explored. The standard is—and has long been—simply this: a scholar breaks new ground, makes a discovery, *advances* the methodology or content of a particular discipline, solves a problem, or clarifies a question in his field, quite often a question that others in his area are laboring day and night, worldwide and competitively, to answer (as, for example, the way Watson discusses the progress of scientific discovery in *The Double Helix*). And these are *objective* contributions, ones that everyone in a given field can agree upon, black, white, or otherwise.

Now, I would do wrong—and I would lie—if I were to suggest that race-related scholarship has no value. On the contrary, this research is profoundly important, particularly in America, where the evolution of this republic—from the moment twenty blacks arrived at Jamestown on a Dutch ship to the triumphs of the Civil Rights Movement—is indebted to countless economic, cultural, and political contributions from people of African descent. Yet, tragically, so much of this marginalized history is, as the late, great Ralph Ellison might put it, still "invisible." Often, when speaking to audiences in America, I ask them to try this imaginative thought experiment: *remove* black people from America's past. Remove them *totally*. What remains? Suddenly, members of the audience realize, after performing this phenomenological variation, that the 244 years of our history that involved the institution of slavery (1619 to 1863), the American Revolution, the Civil War, and U.S. history since Reconstruction become not only hopelessly unintelligible but patently inconceivable.

As a student of (black) American history since the 1960s, I have, therefore, always felt indebted to our scholars who did the difficult, "shoes-in-the-dirt" intellectual labor on which our efforts today rest—outstanding figures such as John Hope Franklin, Zora Neal Hurston (to name but two), and especially that towering genius W. E. B. Du Bois, in whom, if we pause for just a moment to appreciate the magnitude of his achievements, we discover in his life and legacy a prototypical model for the possibilities of men and women of letters in *any* century.

Writer John Oliver Killens did not exaggerate (or at least not by much) when he described Du Bois as "the greatest American intellectual of the twentieth century." His doctoral dissertation *The Suppression of the African Slave Trade to the United States of America, 1638–1870* (1896) remains a canonical study in its field. He followed with equally watershed works of history and sociology, *The Philadelphia Negro* (1899) and *Black Reconstruction in America* (1935)—accomplishments rich enough to constitute a career in themselves, but these publications were only the beginning for his prodigous and protean work in the twentieth century, merely act one for a mind so creatively fertile and expansive that its restlessness, rigor, and most of all singular *vision* inevitably propelled Du Bois into the fields of poetry, fiction, philosophy, cultural criticism, autobiography, and memoir as well as a lifetime of political activism for his people. "His influence as a writer and reformer," said President Nnamdi Azikiwe of Nigeria, "will never diminish." The reason, I believe, for the longevity of Du Bois's oeuvre can be found not solely in the vast content of his contributions, but equally in the motivating spirit, the "fire in the belly" that gave rise to his breathtaking achievements. That spirit is brilliantly on display in his enduring classic *The Souls of Black Folk* (1903), where he writes:

> . . . to make men, we must have ideals, broad, pure, and inspiring ends of living,—not sordid money-getting, not apples of gold. The worker must work for the glory of his handiwork, not simply for pay; the thinker must think for truth, not for fame. And all this is gained only by human strife and longing; by ceaseless training and education; by

founding Right on righteousness and Truth on the unham-
pered search for Truth.

It is clear from these words that Du Bois, like many men of
his era, believed that the work of the mind was, first and foremost, a *moral* work. And that art and scholarship were the fruit
of one's *entire* being, which involved the life of the spirit, the
Feeling Heart (as he phrased it in his 1923 speech "Criteria of
Negro Art"), and the intellect. Compare his words—this wisdom—to a passage in Orestes Brownson's address "The
Scholar's Mission," delivered in 1843 at Dartmouth College:

> I understand by the scholar no mere pedant, dilettante, lit-
> erary epicure or dandy; but a serious, robust, full-grown
> man; who feels that life is a serious affair, and that he has a
> serious part to act in its eventful drama; and must therefore
> do his best to act well his part, so as to leave behind him, in
> the good he has done, a grateful remembrance of his hav-
> ing been. He may be a theologian, a politician, a naturalist,
> a poet, a moralist, or a metaphysician; but whichever or
> whatever he is, he is it with all his heart and soul, with high,
> noble—in one word—*religious* aims and aspirations.

Scholars of the caliber of Du Bois, and our other intellectual
predecesors, would be enormously discouraged, I believe, by the
thinness of black letters today, by our most visible "public intellectuals" allowing themselves to become simply entertainers in
an amusement society, and certainly by the sparse representation of black Americans in the most demanding fields of study.
Yet we must acknowledge that in general, and on the whole, the
American academic zeitgeist is hardly constituted these days to
produce a Du Bois or a William James. Look at the report "The

Dissolution of General Education 1914–1993," released in 1997 by the National Association of Scholars at Princeton, which found that in 1914 almost 90 percent of American colleges made an introductory course in history mandatory—in 1993 only 2 percent of colleges did so. Philosophy courses suffered as well, dropping from more than 75 percent of colleges in 1914 having them as requirements to just 4 percent in 1993.

While I am no fan of author Dinesh D'Souza's book *The End of Racism* (1995), I am convinced we must pay attention to the startling research he presents on the distribution of blacks in fields that require an analytic and quantitative approach to phenomena. His numbers are taken from National Academy Press's *Summary Report 1992: Doctorate Recipients from United States Universities*. There, we discover that in the early 1990s only five black mathematicians were at America's twenty-five top-ranked universities, and that less than 2 percent of this nation's scientists are black. D'Souza, being no friend of black people, pulls no punches. For doctorates earned by various groups in 1992, he provides the following breakdowns:

	Whites	Asians	Hispanics	Blacks	Native Americans
Mathematics	423	51	12	4	2
Computer Science	376	86	8	5	2
Physics and Astronomy	733	92	30	7	6
Chemistry	1,211	132	42	17	6
Engineering	1,874	447	72	48	11
Biological Sciences	3,043	262	101	61	13

D'Souza adds to the depressing numbers above the observation, "Remarkably, nearly one-half of all black doctorates were in a single field, education, with most of the rest in fields like social work and sociology. In a long list of specialized areas, such as algebra, geometry, logic, atomic physics, geophysics, paleontology, oceanography, biomedical engineering, nuclear engineering, cell biology, endocrinology, genetics, microbiology, geography, statistics, classics, comparative literature, archaeology, German language, Italian, Spanish, Russian, accounting, and business economics, in 1992 there were no blacks who earned doctorates in the United States."

The weak black representation in the scientific and technological fields that will dominate the dawn of the twenty-first century tells us that, as a people, our greatest challenge is to create and sustain a new black culture that nurtures a passion for knowledge *for its own sake*. In America, in the past century, black culture has produced an overabundance of athletes and entertainers, indeed, even a surplus of lawyers and people with degrees in the "soft" sciences (ethnology, sociology, psychology); the objective of the *next* century should be, if we are wise, the development of a generation of black scholars capable of speaking with authority and enthusiasm on *any* and *all* subjects that define the human condition. In other words, the responsibility for the intellectual vigor of our lives in the next one hundred years will not rest with a handful of public pundits and spokespersons, but with ourselves. We must establish, culturally, a passion for learning in our children from the moment they are able to speak. In our schools—and in our social lives—we must reward and hold up as role models the eggheads and nerds, the overachievers and driven, type A personalities. Personally, I don't think it would be a bad idea for our churches to create something equivalent to the Jewish bar mitzvah, that coming-of-age ceremony in which a thirteen-year-old boy or girl is publicly embraced as a member of the community, but only after he or she has spent a year in preparation, studying a lengthy section of the Torah that they will be called upon to recite before their congregations, selecting poetry or literature for this event that marks their transition from childhood—in short, doing intellectual and cultural work to earn their respected place among others.

Think about it.

For if we do not rise to this challenge, I fear the world will leave us behind, locked claustrophobically in a parochial study of ourselves, producing book after book with titles prefixed by the word *black*—books that, at the end of the twenty-first century, will be as absent from lists of "the best" as African-American titles are from the Modern Library's recent, revealing inventory.

Uncle Tom's Cabin

I f *Uncle Tom's Cabin* is anything, it is—and has always been—a Rorschach test for a reader's feelings about slavery in general and black people in particular. It is at once both one of the most thoroughly American and piously Christian of major nineteenth-century fictions. In fact, shortly after its publication and within Stowe's lifetime, it transcended the category of literature to become that rarest of products: a cultural artifact; a Rosetta stone for black images in American fiction, theater, and film—not so much a novel, one might say, as an *experience* inseparable from the events that precipitated the Civil War. ("So this," Abraham Lincoln said, famously, when he met Stowe, "is the little lady who wrote the book that made this great war."[1]) It has been the urtext or common coin for discussions about slavery for a century and a half, one woman's very influential interpretation of the Peculiar Institution—an interpretation that we may love or hate, admire or despise, defend or reject, in whole or in part. It is nonetheless a story that so permeates white popular and literary culture, and sits so high astride nineteenth-century American fiction, that it can simply never be ignored.

Given the unique and unparalleled place of *Uncle Tom's Cabin* in our national consciousness, I would suggest that we investigate this novel from two angles. First, we must ask if Stowe's exuberant, panoramic tale succeeds artistically, inquiring into its considerable writerly virtues and lapses of craft. Second, because *Uncle Tom's Cabin* is important not only for what it reveals about the evils of Negro bondage, but also for what it discloses, as W. E. B. DuBois might say, about the "souls of white folk," it is necessary that we read Stowe's brilliant, if hastily written, work in terms of the audience for which it was intended. Her indictment of slavery was written, she confesses, for "generous, noble-minded men and women of the South." We must keep in mind how widely popular this story was with her audience and why. By conservative estimates, the book sold half a million copies within five months of its publication in the United States and later sold just as many in Europe. It inspired, to some extent, the traveling "Tom shows" that toured the South and influenced the Plantation School writers, and probably Margaret Mitchell's 1936 novel, *Gone with the Wind*.

As for its artistry, let me say that *Uncle Tom's Cabin* is far from being a tidy book, either in structure or in content. It suffers, as many nineteenth-century novels did, from what the French call *remplissage* or "literary padding"; improbable plot contrivances (especially the convenient reunion in chapter 42 of once-separated slave families); mawkish sentimentality and unevenness in prose quality, by which I mean a great deal of sententious editorializing and "purple prose" ("Even so, beloved Eva! fair star of thy dwelling! Thou art passing away; but they that love thee dearest know it not"); and the simple need to stretch a story out as long as possible (the aftermath of Eva's death in chapter 27) that plagued fiction published in serial form—in Stowe's case, as forty-five weekly installments in the antislavery paper *The National Era*. (March 20, 1852, was the publication date for the installments as a novel.) Though her novel bears thematic iterations and dramatic redundancies, we should not fault her for these excesses, for it would be another half century before novelists were liberated from the demands of serialization to pursue economy, internal coherence, and a more careful aesthetic design. What *Uncle Tom's Cabin* lacks in concinnity it more than makes up for by being fully imagined and deeply felt.

As a novelist and literary critic, I must confess that I find Stowe's tale, despite its technical flaws, to be an at times impressive, genre-blending amalgam of ahistorical romance, antislavery agitprop, adventure yarn, Dickensian humor, and Christian allegory. The book brims with vivid characters now deeply inscribed in America's racial iconography. (Indeed, these are the very images that I have fought, futilely, to correct and to change for the last thirty years in my own fiction.) It is a classic page-turner, one that masterfully employs the centuries-old strategy of running two story lines simultaneously as it moves back and forth between Eliza's desperate flight north to Canada and Uncle Tom's descent deeper into a life of lesions and lacerations, and finally to his Golgotha on Simon Legree's farm. As we follow their trajectories from Kentucky, Stowe introduces us to a "corps de ballet," as she calls it, that represents a remarkably broad slice of America's population in the mid nineteenth century, Northerners and Southerners, women and men, aristocratic and lower-class whites, and a diversity of house and field servants.

There is the mulatto genius George Harris, inventor of a hemp-cleaning machine, who, like Frederick Douglass, was forced to compete with his master's dogs for bones to feed himself. We meet his light-skinned wife, Eliza, whose escape across cakes of ice on the Ohio River, her child Henry in her arms, is an image of slavery that will forever haunt America's imagination. Stowe's generosity in giving us a universe of human beings to care about and contemplate is nothing short of astonishing. She offers us, for example, not one but *three* deliciously wicked scalawags, the first being Dan Haley, a lubricious slave trader who would probably sell his own mother for a profit. Yet in one incident of legerdemain that must have delighted novelist Ralph Ellison, Stowe derails Haley's pursuit of Eliza with the hilarious *bobservations* of Mr. Shelby's slave Sam, a man who knows "which side the bread is buttered on." The other two bottom feeders are Marks and Tom Loker, both wonderfully sketched Fagins transplanted to an American landscape; but Stowe, ever the evangelist, promises even these severely tainted souls a taste of redemption when Loker's heart is softened by Quakers who nurse him after a nasty fall. And that, of course, is the relentless message of Stowe's narrative—that *all* can be redeemed by Christian love. Even the despised and pathetic black imp Topsy, who believes "I's so wicked!" until Miss Ophelia (one of this novel's finest and most convincing creations) overcomes her prejudice against Negroes to become a New England Pygmalion to this child's Nubian Galatea.

On and on, Stowe fills her capacious novel with intriguing types and stereotypes: the half-mad Cassy, enslaved to Legree, a moral monster lusting after fifteen-year-old Emmeline; the guilt-ridden Augustine St. Clare, his hypochondriac wife, Marie, and their impossibly innocent, Shirley Temple look-alike daughter, Eva, whom Stowe uses badly and baldly as the most sanctimonious mouthpiece for abolition. And then, of course, there is the now controversial (though not in 1852) figure of

Uncle Tom, a gentle, profoundly religious slave who is always the spiritual and moral superior of the three white men who successively own him.

So, yes, pure storytelling is alive, well, and truly vibrant on these pages from the antebellum era. We cannot stop reading until, by heaven, we know what hand destiny, in the form of Harriet Beecher Stowe, deals them. What will become of Eliza and George? Will Uncle Tom *ever* be reunited with his family as a free man? A contemporary writer experiences Stowe's bottomless talent for invention with just a twinge of professional envy.

However, we also find on these pages a portrait of black people that, from a twenty-first-century perspective, is ineluctably racist. And truly beyond salvage. Stowe is at pains to present an attractive image of blacks, arguing that the African is as fully human as the Anglo-Saxon, a point that surely needed to be driven home again and again and yet again to whites in her time (and for a century thereafter). However, Stowe's interpretation of the "nature" of Negroes is her novel's central and most self-destructive flaw. It simply replaces one racist stereotype with another that is equally condescending and unacceptable. Yet it is a flaw, a lack of epistemological humility, that teaches us much about the trouble white Americans typically have with understanding the racial or cultural Other *in his own terms*. (This is now a problem that American "infidels" have, hugely, with understanding Islam and the Middle East after September 11, 2001.)

In at least fifteen authorial proclamations, Stowe breathlessly informs her readers that blacks are "naturally patient, timid and unenterprising." They are affectionate, have an indigenous talent for cooking, and are more moved by religious feeling than the Anglo-Saxon because "unquestioning faith . . . is more a native element to this race than any other." Their kind nature is "ever yearning toward the simple and childlike," which is exactly how

Stowe describes Eva and that emasculated black "behemoth" of a man, Uncle Tom, when these two are together—as both being lovable children. Augustine St. Clare, for his part, is as amused by Topsy as he would be by "a parrot or a pointer." For this nineteenth-century author, Negro slavery is wrong because it brutalizes a race that is by nature as harmless as a beloved house pet. There is nothing to fear in them. And it is the duty, she argues, of the more sophisticated and bold white race to gently lead the Negro as the parent does the child; as Mrs. Shelby says she did the "poor, simple creatures" on her Kentucky farm; and as Miss Ophelia does Topsy.

In Western, white humanity's painfully slow progress toward social enlightenment, Stowe's now embarrassing, unfortunately toxic racial thinking is a small step forward, from hatred and negrophobia to a blatant paternalism that was used soon enough to rationalize colonialism and, we must admit, exists to this very day. Her understanding of black people contains, at best, two parts truth and eight parts error. But while we may wince at her brand of half-blind progressivism, it *was* a change for the better. In 1852, she could not fully see that the very concept of "race" was a chimera—a collective delusion created in the eighteenth century to justify white social, political, and economic domination. She and her abolitionist husband, Calvin E. Stowe, met slaves and even used their Ohio home as a "station" for the Underground Railroad, but it is patently clear that this very well-meaning and risk-taking writer never knew black people *in their own terms*.

Her dramatic argument against Negro bondage after the alarming passage of the Fugitive Slave Act of 1850 demands, for example, that one believe that whites like Simon Legree inflict violence and humiliation upon blacks, but not vice versa. (Notice how George Harris *wounds* but does not kill Loker, and it is a white man, not the fleeing slaves, who pushes the bounty hunter into a chasm.) Thus, she dare not even hint in her novel at the numerous slave revolts that took place on American soil—the Stono Rebellion, or Nat Turner's bloody rampage.[2] While Augustine St. Clare mentions to his brother Alfred the insurrection in "Hayti," he stops short of revealing that blacks led by the voodoo priest Boukman and Toussaint L'Ouverture killed every white man, woman, and child on France's former colonial possession, thereby so frustrating Napoleon's imperialistic ambitions in the New World that he sold New Orleans and vast amounts of the surrounding land to Thomas Jefferson for 60 million francs (about $15 million) in the Louisiana Purchase, a deal that greatly expanded the young nation's territory. Never, wrote historian Henry Adams, "did the United States government get so much for so little."[3]

Stowe doubts that her black characters, if they remain on American soil, can create a culture of their own—one not derived from or dependent upon Christianity or Europe, in other words, one not based on what white people think and do. For that, they must leave this country. Whether she realized it or not, her sense of American blacks is always that of relative beings who, if they are noble like Uncle Tom, are worthy of freedom and respect only because they so perfectly mirror the values and ideals that their white oppressors made claims to but nevertheless betrayed. Well might her Southern readers, as they wept over Uncle Tom's death, have agreed with a white lady who once said of her servant, "I can not meet him in society, but I hope to meet him in heaven." Stowe speculates that one day "Africa shall show an elevated and cultivated race—and come it must, some time, her turn to figure in the great drama of human improvement, life will awaken there with a gorgeousness and splendor of which our cold western tribes faintly have conceived." Apparently Stowe knows nothing of the achievements of the Ghana, Mali, and Songhay empires during Europe's Dark Ages. That aside, it is Stowe's very tentative hypothesis that so disturbed Charles Dickens. In a letter dated July 17, 1852, he chided her for going "too far." "I doubt there being any warrant," he said, "for making out the African race to be a great race, or for supposing the future destinies of the world to lie in that direction; and I think this extreme championship likely to repel some useful sympathy and support."[4]

One wants to ask Dickens, repel *whom?* Well, clearly, he means the thousands of white readers of *Uncle Tom's Cabin*. Dickens overlooks the fact that in Stowe's America, one popular and "compassionate" solution to the question of what to *do* with freed slaves was to train them, then send them all back to Africa, specifically to Liberia, which was created for exactly that purpose. Deporting ex-slaves to Africa took the form of policy on January 1, 1817, with the formation of the American Colonization Society, a creation of Robert Finley that was endorsed with enthusiasm by President James Madison and former president Thomas Jefferson. "I go to *my country*—my chosen, my glorious Africa!" proclaims George Harris in the novel's antepenultimate chapter, sounding more than a little like Paul Cuffe, a free Philadelphia businessman who in 1811 founded in Sierra Leone the Friendly Society for the emigration of blacks to Africa. Topsy goes there, too, as a missionary. And Cassy's son. Like Stowe, Abraham Lincoln supported repatriation of Negroes to Africa, a separation of the races that would solve the "Negro problem," as it was called as late as the 1950s, and leave America undiluted as a white man's country. Not once does it occur to them that American history on every level imaginable—political, economic, and cultural—is inconceivable without the presence of black people on this continent from the time of the seventeenth-century colonies. That, in other words, their deeds and contributions have made black people as "American" as any white person, and perhaps more American than many.

Finally, it must be noted that, while *Uncle Tom's Cabin* demonstrates rousing narrative skill, it willfully soft-pedals (or ignores) much of slavery's real sadism and surrealism. ("What man has nerve to do, man has not nerve to hear," demurs Stowe decorously.) Although chapter 31 is whimsically titled "Middle Passage," Stowe does not touch upon the nightmarish voyage that 20 million Africans took, crammed belly to buttocks, spoon-fashion, in the holds of slave ships in which 20 percent of their number died before reaching the New World. Her depictions of slavery's horrors are, if compared to the historical record, merely the iceberg's tip of two hundred years of depravity and cruelty inflicted on Africans in a Kafkaesque social system that was, by any standard, insane. Slavery is as old as mankind, yes. (We owe the word *slave* itself to the Slavs, who were forced into bondage in Europe and the Ottoman Empire.) We find it practiced among all peoples, and at all times. It exists today in the war-torn Sudan where for five hundred dollars, the cash equivalent of five cows, you can purchase another human being.

But what put the *peculiar* in the "Peculiar Institution" was the superimposition of white-supremacist ideology onto the enslavement of blacks by WASPs who employed all the Manichaean symbolism of difference between "white" (good) and "black" (evil) found in the Judeo-Christian tradition (dating back at least to Plotinus) to portray people of color as inherently inferior and to justify their total subjugation. Stowe's benign slave owners like St. Clare are tormented by the transparency of this lie; by the schizophrenia of desiring slavery's profitability and at the same time believing that all men are created equal;

and by the nagging sense that not only have whites lived an illusion since 1619 when the first Africans arrived at Jamestown, but what is even worse, if their religion is right, they have condemned their own souls and those of their children to eternal damnation. (This novel, said James Baldwin, "is activated by what might be called a theological terror, the terror of damnation."⁵) It is this electrifying "moral" or, if you prefer, Christian clarity regarding the evils of slavery and racism that *Uncle Tom's Cabin* injected for the first time into the discourse of white America, and in that lies the mixed, partial triumph of Harriet Beecher Stowe's most famous book.

One hundred and fifty years after its publication, *Uncle Tom's Cabin* can still serve us, though not in the way that Stowe and her admirers intended. It invites us to discuss whether a white author can successfully portray a black person *in his own terms,* instead of through the distorting, fun-house mirror of white, Eurocentric ideas about people of color. I have studied white depictions of those of African descent in American culture now for half a century, and not *once* in fifty years have I seen the complexity and multifaceted character of my people rendered by white authors in a way I could honestly identify with, or find compelling for its fidelity and veracity. Don't get me wrong. Admirable attempts have been made by whites to "capture" the racial Other. For example, Sinclair Lewis talked with and carefully listened to black people, as well as studied the files of the NAACP in the 1940s, before he wrote *Kingsblood Royal.* The rich, cultural diversity of the world in which we live demands that we, as writers, forever strive—with empathy and epistemological humility—to grasp something of the Other's *Lebenswelt* or "Life-world," as phenomenologists put it, and always with the understanding that what we think we "know" is highly provisional. If one works in this spirit, I think it is possible for the white portraits of blacks to be at least inoffensive and tentatively "right enough," which is how my friend critic John Whalen-Bridge described the best of such efforts. But for genuine insights into African-American lives I know I must turn to the work of black authors themselves. Stowe's book challenges us today to ask whether it is possible ever to write well the lived experience of the racial Other. And for that reason, if none other, her novel deserves attention at this dawn of a new millennium.

The Singular Vision of
Ralph Ellison

What on earth was hiding behind the face of things?" the Everyman narrator of *Invisible Man* asks himself in Ralph Ellison's perennial masterpiece. His unique dilemma, and ours, is the formidable task of freeing himself from the blinding social illusions that render races and individuals invisible to each other. Only after a harrowing, roller-coaster ride of betrayals and revelations above and below America's twentieth-century intellectual landscape does he achieve the liberating discovery that, for all the ideologies we impose upon experience, we cannot escape the chaos, the mysterious, untamed life that churns beneath official history, the "seen," and ensures the triumph of the imagination.

By any measure, *Invisible Man* is the most complex, multilayered, and challenging novel about race and being and the preservation of democratic ideals in American literature. Fellow writers read Ellison with awe and gratitude. Some, of course, read him with jealousy, because everything one could want in a novel is here: humor, suspense, black history (that is, American history) from which Ellison's inexhaustible imagination teases forth truth from beneath mere facts, fuguelike prose, meditations on the nature of perception, and a rogues' gallery of characters so essentially drawn that in their naked humanity we can recognize their spirits in our contemporaries fifty years after the book's publication.

Added to that, and perhaps most impressive of all, Ellison's expansive rite of passage is the very idea of artistic generosity. Its exuberant, Hegelian movements gracefully blend diverse literary genres and traditions, from Mark Twain to William Faulkner, from the slave narrative to the surrealistic Kafkaesque parable, from black folklore to Freud, forever forcing us to see in the novel's technique the spirit of democracy. Spanning South and North, it traces the comic progress of a nameless black student from a state college aswim in the contradictions of Booker T. Washington's reliance on white philanthropy, to New York, where Marxists and black nationalists are engaged in a Harlem turf war.

And, as if this were not enough, Ellison gave our age a new metaphor for social alienation. His definition of "invisibility" is so common now, so much a part of the culture and language—like a coin handled by billions—that it is automatically invoked when we talk about the situation of American blacks, and for *any* social group we willingly refuse to see.

In the late 1960s when I was a college student and came of age in an anti-intellectual climate thick with separatist arguments for the necessity of a "black aesthetic," when both Ellison and poet Robert Hayden were snubbed by those under the spell of black cultural nationalism, and when so many black critics denied the idea of "universality" in literature and life, I stumbled upon *Invisible Man* and spent three memorable nights not so much reading as dreaming, absorbing, and being altered by his remarkable adventure of ideas and artistic possibility, though I knew—at age twenty—I was missing far more than I grasped.

But each time I returned to Ellison's overrich book, teaching the novel many times over twenty-five years, I found new imaginative and intellectual portals to enter, more layers of meaning to peel away. Of the thousands of American novels I have read, his has been the most reliable guide for giving a young writer full access to his ethnicity and his Yankeeness. The social and spiritual dangers depicted in *Invisible Man*, the various forms of self-inflicted "blindness," and the intricacies of racial collision are so exhaustively treated in this single, metamorphic machine of a book that every ten years or so we are obliged to check our cultural progress and failures against its admonitions.

Despite his groundbreaking achievements, the awards with which he was showered when *Invisible Man* was published, and the direction his work gave to a generation of black writers who came of age in the 1960s, Ellison's novel has often presented too severe an intellectual and moral challenge for readers reluctant to abandon simplistic formulas about race in America. Indeed, his book once inspired rage. In his 1952 review, writer John Oliver Killens said, "The Negro people need Ralph Ellison's *Invisible Man* like we need a hole in the head or a stab in the back. . . . It is a vicious distortion of Negro life." Equally critical was Amiri Baraka, who dismissed Ellison as a middle-class Negro for his insistence that mastery of literary craft must take priority over politics in a writer's apprenticeship. For Ellison that apprenticeship included T. S. Eliot as well as Langston Hughes, Pound and Hemingway alongside Richard Wright, Gertrude Stein and Dostoyevsky together with the blues.

* * *

Fortunately, *Invisible Man* can also be enjoyed on the level of rousing entertainment, as a thrilling odyssey that follows a naive but ambitious young man through an entire universe of unforgettable characters and events. There is Mr. Norton, one of the white founders of a black college—"a trustee of consciousness"—who believes Negroes are his "fate" and discovers his deepest fears and desires mirrored back at him by Jim Trueblood, a black sharecropper who has committed incest. No less startling is Dr. Bledsoe, the sinister administrator of a school that features a "bronze statue of the college Founder, the cold Father symbol, his hands outstretched in the breathtaking gesture of lifting a veil that flutters in hand, metallic folds above the face of a kneeling slave; and I stand puzzled," says Ellison's protagonist, "unable to decide whether the veil is really being lifted, or lowered more firmly in place; whether I am witnessing a revelation or a more efficient blinding."

On and on they come: mythic characters spun from the social paradoxes of the uniquely American belief in (and failure to achieve) equality—Lucius Brockway, the black laborer installed in the bowels of Liberty Paints, the "machine within the machine"; Brother Jack, leader of an organization dedicated to "working for a better world for all people," but racist to its core and eager to eliminate people "like dead limbs that must be pruned away" if they fail to serve the group's purpose; and Ras the Exhorter, a Harlem demagogue encapsulating in one powerful figure Afrocentric thought from Marcus Garvey to Malcolm X to, even today, Leonard Jeffries ("You t'ink I'm crazy, it is c'ase I speak bahd English? Hell, it ain't my mama tongue, mahn. I'm African")—all of them blind, Ellison says, to his protagonist's humanity, his individuality, and the synthetic, creolizing process long at work in this country, making each and every one of us, whether we like it or not, a cultural mongrel.

That underlying experience, which so many in the universe of *Invisible Man* fail to see, is delivered by Ellison in several astonishing scenes most novelists would give their firstborn children to have created. One is the cryptic paint factory episode, where "Optic White" is mixed with ten drops of black "dope," which is expected to disappear into the "purest white that can be found," but instead reveals a "gray tinge"—a blending of the two into one that changes the identity of both. Another is the masterful Harlem eviction scene in which the possessions of an old black couple thrown onto the street become a doorway for experiencing black history from the Civil War forward. A third, the most striking episode of all, is the Rinehart section, at once hilarious and profound as it dramatizes the polymorphous character of human seeing, the fluidity of the self, and portrays "history" as a mental construct beyond which lies "a world . . . without boundaries."

As might be expected, appreciating the achievement of Ellison's fiction inevitably means taking seriously both the singular aesthetic position that makes it possible and his notion of the Negro's crucial role in this country's evolution—an understanding shared by most of our elders born early in the century.

Read his 1981 introduction to *Invisible Man*. In that essay, Ellison confronts, then triumphantly solves, a problem that had long haunted the fiction of a young nation known for the strong anti-intellectual strains in its culture. It is "the question of why most protagonists of Afro-American fiction (not to mention the black characters in fiction by whites) were without intellectual depth. Too often they were figures caught up in the most intense forms of social struggle, subject to the most extreme forms of the human predicament but yet seldom able to articulate the issues which tortured them."

However, his happy (for us) discovery, one that everyone concerned about "multiculturalism" would do well to memorize, was that, "by a trick of fate (and our racial problems notwithstanding), *the human imagination is integrative—and the same is true of the centrifugal force that inspirits the democratic process.*" (Italics mine.)

Such an insight enabled him to envision and execute the visionary work that has been part of our literary canon for forty years. In theorizing about it, he said, "I would have to provide him [Invisible Man] with something of a worldview, give him a consciousness in which serious philosophical questions could be raised, provide him with a range of diction that could play upon the richness of our readily shared vernacular speech . . . and of American types as they operated on various levels of society."

Hoping to create "a fiction which, leaving sociology to the scientists, arrived at the truth about the human condition, here and now, with all the bright magic of a fairy tale," Ellison devoted seven years to the novel's execution. His theory led him into lasting insights, edging him toward a way to sing the unseen so often in the novel that even his casual asides cannot be ignored, as when Invisible Man thinks of his literature class, where he studied James Joyce, and his teacher observes:

"Stephen's problem, like ours, was not actually one of creating the uncreated conscience of his race, but of creating the *uncreated features of his face.* Our task is that of making ourselves individuals. The conscience of a race is the gift of its individuals who see, evaluate, record. . . . We create the race by creating ourselves and then to our great astonishment we will have created something far more important: We will have created a culture. Why waste time creating a conscience for something that doesn't exist? For, you see, blood and skin do not think!" Because no author could hope for more than to work in this wonderful,

Ellisonesque spirit of inclusion, I dedicated my acceptance speech for the National Book Award in fiction to Ralph Ellison when my third novel, *Middle Passage*, won that prize in 1990. It seemed to me the very least I could do in the presence of an elder who had forged a place in American culture for the possibility of the fiction I dreamed of writing. For a man who, when the global list of the most valuable authors of the twentieth century is finally composed, will be among those at the pinnacle.

On *Kingsblood Royal*

In "A Note About *Kingsblood Royal*," a 1947 essay published in *Wings*, the Literary Guild review, Sinclair Lewis, the first American to receive the Nobel Prize in literature (1930), made the following observations:

> I don't think the Negro Problem is insoluble because I don't think there is any Negro Problem. . . . There are no distinctive colored persons. The mad, picture-puzzle idiocy of the whole theory of races is beautifully betrayed when you get down to the question of "Negroes" who are white enough to pass as Caucasians. . . . There was a time in our history, and ever so short a time ago, when the Scotch-English in New England thought all the Irish were fundamentally different and fundamentally inferior. And then those same conceited Yanks (my own people) moved on to the Middle West and went through the same psychological monkey-shines with the Scandinavians and the Bohemians and the

Poles. None of the profound and convincing nonsense of race difference can be made into sense.[1]

Lewis's twentieth novel, published that same year, reads like a raging dramatization of this declaration: namely, that what we have always had in America is a White Problem, not a Negro one. In his story, set in 1945, Neil Kingsblood is a thirty-one-year-old former infantry captain and a junior bank officer living a comfortable, privileged, and blind life in a segregated community, Sylvan Park, in Grand Republic, Minnesota. Like all his relatives, neighbors, and friends, Kingsblood is a digest of racial misinformation, prejudice, and white arrogance, although his ignorance seems almost innocent—a *received* bigotry picked up from others, like a cold. That is, until his dentist father confides in Neil that their unusual last name is possibly a sign of royal blood and asks him to look into the matter. Neil does, researching his father's lineage, but finds no English kings. Then he traces his mother's roots to an eighteenth-century ancestor, Xavier Pic. Thus begins the unraveling of Neil Kingsblood's life. Pic, he learns, was "a full-blooded Negro." Psychologically, Neil lurches from horror, fearing especially for his daughter's future, to questioning everything he'd heard about blacks, to the decision of saying nothing about his one thirty-second inheritance from Pic, and finally to a full unlocking of his perceptions of the social world. Being "black" suddenly forces Kingsblood to develop a complex inner life, a rich, questioning subjectivity that reads all the objects and others of his former "white" world with a critical acuity he did not before possess. For this ontological liberation, this apostasy from whiteness, Neil is thankful: "What a clack-mouthed parrot I was! I think God turned me black to save my soul, if I have any beyond ledgers and college yells."

His soul is soon tested when Kingsblood announces his

new identity to black friends he makes after his self-discovery, Negroes who are (except for one Uncle Tom and a few called "bad medicine") the very portrait of dignity, individualism, decency, intelligence, and compassion—hitherto unknown residents of Grand Republic whose company Neil comes to *prefer* when his own family (except for his wife, Vestal, his daughter, Biddy, and his sister, Pat) react hysterically to the uncovering of their black ancestry, and his erstwhile friends, each revealing a foulness of spirit, make him a pariah. Kingsblood learns racial oppression firsthand, enduring insults and unemployment. But when a racist organization called Sant Tabac ("Stop all Negro trouble, take action before any comes") begins driving blacks from Grand Republic and Kingsblood's execrable neighbors attempt to evict *him* from their community, he and his new black friends take up arms against a white mob in the novel's final scene. Race traitor Captain Kingsblood has, in effect, returned to "the great gray republic" from fighting one war in Europe to find himself again battling fascism, but this time right in his own backyard.

All in all, *Kingsblood Royal* is a perennially astonishing book, for Lewis, a chronicler of American life since 1912, deploys the full range of his satirical and mimetic gifts, his naturalist's fidelity to detail, and his amazingly careful research into black life to exhaustively catalog the entire gamut of WASP practices and toxic sociological fantasies. Honesty demands we acknowledge that Lewis absorbed more African-American history than most blacks knew in 1947 (and probably know today). And, as if this were not enough, he writes with such devastatingly accurate insights into the absurdity of what W. E. B. Du Bois called the twentieth century's central problem, "the color line," that after fifty-four years *Kingsblood Royal* reads as if it might well have been written yesterday—and by someone with a master's degree in black studies. No less noteworthy is the fact that this savage novel appeared at the very moment Americans concluded, with much self-congratulation, a world war to stop the greatest "race man" of all time, Adolf Hitler, and a full generation before the color-blind Civil Rights Movement inspired blacks and whites to challenge Northern enclaves of bigotry and middle-class banality like Grand Republic (also the setting for 1945's *Cass Timberlane*).

Yet while this book follows a template Lewis developed in earlier novels such as *Main Street* and *Babbitt*—the story of an idealistic "insider" gradually transformed into a nonconforming social rebel who exposes some form of hypocrisy in American culture—it must be judged, in the final analysis, as less a novel than a corrosively effective polemic. Composed in roughly sixteen months, with a first draft done in only five,[2] *Kingsblood Royal* has the feel of a barn-burning tract, a crusading indictment of the racial rot festering just beneath the deceptively placid surface of any American community. His characters are one-dimensional caricatures, the plot is more episodic than energetic, and Kingsblood's "coming out" is risible because he has so little African blood a mosquito might extract all of it with one bite. But even though it is flawed and failed as a fully realized work of fiction, it succeeded in shocking the million and a half readers of *Kingsblood Royal* from their midcentury racial slumbers (*Ebony* magazine awarded Lewis a plaque for the book of the year that did the most to improve interracial understanding), and it added a new dimension to the novel of "passing" established as a literary subgenre by two generations of distinguished black American authors.

Critic Robert E. Fleming, in his 1986 article "*Kingsblood Royal* and the Black 'Passing' Novel," discusses Lewis's book in terms of several important literary antecedents that explored this subject, among them William Wells Brown's *Clotel, or The President's Daughter* (1853), James Weldon Johnson's *The Autobiography of an Ex-Coloured Man* (1912), Jessie Fauset's *Plum Bun* (1928), and Nella Larsen's *Passing* (1929), as well as works by white authors: William Dean Howells's *An Imperative Duty* (1892) and Mark Twain's *Pudd'nhead Wilson* (1894).[3] According to Fleming, Sinclair Lewis knew both Johnson, with whom he sometimes corresponded, and novelist Walter White, an executive (like Johnson) of the National Association for the Advancement of Colored People, who introduced him to "prominent black intellectuals" and supplied him "with material from the files of the NAACP when Lewis was working on *Kingsblood Royal*." In addition to this direct debt to black authors and activists, Fleming refers to an article by critic Charles F. Cooney, who speculated that Neil Kingsblood may "to a limited extent . . . have been based on Walter White, who once was referred to by Lewis as a 'voluntary' Negro." (In *Great Negroes Past and Present*, White is described as a "blue-eyed, pink-skinned Negro with reddish hair," a description identical to Kingsblood.[4])

Fleming notes the striking similarities between *Kingsblood Royal* and *The Autobiography of an Ex-Coloured Man*; indeed, he finds the influence of Johnson's classic work to be "pervasive" insofar as both novels begin in the supposedly less prejudiced North, both feature protagonists who trace their black ancestry through their mothers, both hold blacks in contempt before their moments of racial revelation, and both have "an intellectual acquaintance whose worth is recognized only after the protagonist discovers his own black heritage." Despite his clear indebtedness to black literature, Lewis's book, concludes Fleming, is "a thorough updating of an important theme in American literature."

One final observation by Lewis deserves our attention. "Actually," he wrote in his 1947 essay, "the 'race question' is only a small part of *Kingsblood Royal*, but it is the part that will stand out." When Lewis, whose earlier works critically examined a variety of twentieth-century institutions such as the medical profession (*Arrowsmith*), organized religion (*Elmer Gantry*), big business (*Dodsworth*), American fascism (*It Can't Happen Here*), and social welfare (*Ann Vickers*), thought about Neil Kingsblood, he saw a young man whose "romantic and rather terrifying courage" had not been blunted by "the banal slickness of electric refrigerators and tiled bathrooms and convertible coupes," in other words, all the detritus of contemporary lives mired in conformity, lies, materialism, hatred, and anti-intellectualism. He believed "it makes sense to see and try to understand a young man like my hero, kindly, devoted to bridge and hunting, fond of his pleasant wife and adorable daughter, who flies off the handle and suddenly decides that certain social situations, which he had never thought of before, were intolerable. In order to fight those situations, with a grimness and a valor probably greater than that of any fancy medieval knight, not hysterically, but with a quiet and devastating anger, he risks his job, his social caste, his good repute, his money, and the father and mother and wife and child whom he loves."

That "terrifying courage" of the individual confronting the tyranny and torpidity of the tribe is constantly held up for admiration in his oeuvre and, for Sinclair Lewis, is the deeper—and perhaps truly universal—meaning of *Kingsblood Royal*.

Progress in Literature

What a writer in our time has to do is write what hasn't been written before or beat dead men at what they have done.

—Ernest Hemingway

At the dawn of the twenty-first century we are now so accustomed to reading every week about astonishing advances in such fields as medicine and technology that evidence for "progress" in the sciences, theoretical and applied, is inescapable. Consider for a moment just a few of the scientific endeavors of a single year, 1999: two independent teams of astronomers at four institutions announced the discovery of the first multiplanet system around a normal star (Upsilon Andromedae) other than our own; in August, November, and January 2000, NASA's spacecraft *Galileo,* launched in 1989, made its closest-ever flybys of Jupiter's moons—Thebe, Almalthea and Metis—transmitting back images and information from 386 million miles away; research teams in Europe and the United States reported the successful decoding of DNA for a complete plant chromosome while scientists at the University of Washington's Department of Molecular Biotechnology announced they had mapped roughly 85 percent of the genetic code for rice; in Tokyo, scientist Makoto Asashima and his research team grew frog ears and eyes in a laboratory, using the animal's embryo cells; New York's Dobelle Institute, a medical device company, premiered in January 2000 a device that enabled a sixty-two-year-old blind man to read large letters and move around objects courtesy of a tiny camera—an artificial eye—wired directly to his brain; PPL Therapeutics in Edinburgh, Scotland, the company that cloned Dolly the sheep, followed that groundbreaking event by cloning five piglets.

Few would doubt that one essential feature of life in the twenty-first century—perhaps *the* dominant, dizzying, and often Faustian characteristic—is exponential growth and inexorable change in man's ability to quantify, manipulate, and diagram life's material dimensions—from measuring the climate on Mars to charting human DNA in the Genome Project. Science triumphs by painstaking methods developed over two millennia: the apodictic rigor of mathematics, a correspondence theory of truth, predictability, precise measurements calculated in nanoseconds (the oscillations of the cesium atom), intersubjective observations capable of being confirmed by researchers all over the globe, regardless of their cultural backgrounds, and a demand for (ever increasing) empirical evidence that renders the conclusions and products of but a few months ago obsolete and current knowledge provisional.

But what of literature? Can the term *progress* be applied to a field that, traditionally in the West since the time of Plato, falls into the category of the subjective, the culturally (and racially) relative, the unquantifiable, and is everywhere dominated by unpredictable emotional responses, shifting opinions, the vagaries of "taste" and personal preference? The apparent absurdity (and I will argue it is *only* apparent) of speaking about "progress" in the arts can be best illustrated by asking, hypothetically, if one artistic work ever disproves, replaces, refutes, or refines another as, say, Copernicus's heliocentric science proved to be less cumbersome and complicated than Ptolemy's geocentrism and Kant's analysis of consciousness proved to be a more convincing account than the earlier one presented by David Hume? If, for example, Richard Wright's *Native Son* was rendered obsolete twelve years later by Ralph Ellison's *Invisible Man*, or if a canvas by Jackson Pollock "disproves" one by Pablo Picasso? The criteria we apply to the sciences seem to fail the instant they are applied to the arts. Yet we would err, and we would do wrong, if we concluded that "progress" is not evident in the evolution of literary practice.

To illustrate this point we need look no further than the relatively recent history of the English novel, which as a distinctive narrative art is dated by many, if not most, critics to 1739 when Samuel Richardson published his "novel of character," *Pamela.* (Some critics, we should note, argue instead for Daniel Defoe's "novel of incident" *Robinson Crusoe* in 1719 and *Moll Flanders* in 1722.) Storytelling—in the forms of the epic, the drama, and the lyric—is, of course, an activity as old as humankind. But in *An Outline of the Novel* (1965) Richard M. Eastman persuasively argues that prose narratives premiered in continental literature as late medieval romances, tales of knights and their adventures (the term for the novel in most European languages is *roman*, indicating its ancestry in *romance*).[1] By the early Renaissance, popular narratives presented short, prose tales of common life (Boccaccio) in common language and came to be known by the Italian word *novella* or "little new thing," from which comes our English word *novel.* Among the "proto-novels" before the eighteenth century, Eastman identifies Malory's *Morte d'Arthur* (1485), and Cervantes's *Don Quixote* (1605–15), and to these important predecessors we can add picaresque fiction (the episodic tales of rogues or "picaros").

Those earlier works, Eastman explains, developed narrative strategies later useful for the singular design of the novel as we know it, but its essential architecture could not properly emerge until after three cultural transformations had taken place. (1) The epistemological revolution fathered by Descartes, Bacon, and Locke, whose works presented a new, inductive science privileging no longer the deductive methods of medieval school-men but instead an individual consciousness that experienced and confirmed "reality" through the senses, a development that stimulated in the 1600s and 1700s the unique European passion for recording individual experience at a specific time and place, for biographies, autobiographies, letters, and the field of journalism itself. (2) The Protestant Reformation, which in the 1500s encouraged universal literacy by emphasizing each individual Christian's direct relationship to God and the importance of reading the Bible. And (3) the end of feudalism, which saw the rise of an energetic, bourgeoisie class that supported the publishing trade and hungered for a new literature capable of portraying its struggles (not those of an aristocracy) and revealing the geography of the natural world this class was eager to explore.

No form satisfied those challenges quite as well as the novel, a long narrative that drew its defining characteristics from Defoe's journalistic attention to the surface detail of contemporary life; from Henry Fielding's sense of Aristotelian unity, his familiarity with Restoration drama, and his sensitivity to diverse voices and vernaculars and social manners in *Tom Jones;* and from Laurence Sterne's realization of the possibilities for small, epiphanic moments or events disclosing a character to his depths in *Tristram Shandy*.

Based on this eighteenth-century archetype, the novel was able to undergo infinite variations on its basic paradigm, expanding its range of subjects (*all* phenomenal experience was its subject), absorbing countless other forms such as the epic, romance and allegory, and creating for itself subgenres. (As experimental novelist Ishmael Reed once remarked, "A novel can be the six o'clock news," a point proven earlier in the 1930s when John Dos Passos sprinkled documentary-like "newsreels" throughout his epic *U.S.A.* trilogy.) By the late nineteenth century, which saw in Europe the emergence of the philosophies of positivism and naturalism, the novel's "realistic" foundations permitted even greater efforts to achieve a more "scientific" rendering of human affairs (think of Flaubert's *Madame Bovary*), efforts that were informed by the new fields of psychology and sociology. As it exists today, the novel's *eidos*—or essence—necessarily includes the presence, to a lesser or greater degree, of the character, plot, and structural features established by its eighteenth-century practitioners, the naturalistic refinements it experienced in the nineteenth, and a "psychological realism" that emerged in the early twentieth. Its fundamental design has not significantly changed in three centuries. However, we should not see this as a rigid *formula*. To better understand this distinction between *form* and *formula* it would be helpful if we looked at the history of a related form: the modern short story.

As mentioned previously, storytelling is ancient, with written examples reaching back to the Egyptians' "The Tales of the Magicians," which possibly date from 4000 B.C.[2] The *tale* was attractive, as a form, to writers as diverse as Geoffrey Chaucer, Nathaniel Hawthorne, and Washington Irving; within its long tradition we find other forms of short prose—the sketch, apologue, parable, anecdote, vignette, and fable, to name but a few. In May of 1842, in *Graham's Magazine*, Edgar Allan Poe published a review of Hawthorne's *Twice-Told Tales* entitled, "On the Aim and Technique of the Short Story," and in that brilliant essay—as well as in his own work—defined the modern short story as a form distinct from the novel, novella, and other kinds of short prose. Poe asserted that the short prose narrative should require "from a half-hour to one or two hours" to read. Furthermore, he insisted that its writer

> having conceived, with deliberate care, a certain unique or single *effect* to be wrought out, he then invents such incidents—he then combines such events as may best aid him in establishing this preconceived effect. If his very initial sentence tends not to the outbringing of this effect, then he has failed in his first step. In the whole composition there should be no word written, of which the tendency, direct or indirect, is not to the one pre-established design.

Clearly, the novel can not be read in two hours or convey but a single emotional effect. Poe stressed the importance of "invention, creation, imagination, and originality." To his demand that *every* word reinforce that overall effect, Poe added in another essay, "The Philosophy of Composition" (1846), that "it is only with the *denouement* constantly in view that we can give a plot its indispensable air of consequence, of causation, by making the incidents, and especially the tone at all points, tend to the development of the intention." And in yet a third essay on Hawthorne, published in 1847, Poe condemns his use of allegory, saying, "If allegory ever established a fact, it is by dint of overturning a fiction." What emerged from the theory and practice of this nineteenth-century genius, who has been credited with inventing the modern short story, was a craft that judged all examples of this form's success by its "unity of effect."

Others built upon Poe's insights, among them critic Brander Matthews, who, in his essay "The Philosophy of the Short-Story" (1901), attempted to give an even more precise definition: "The Short-story fulfills the three false unities of French classic drama: it shows one action, in one place, on one day. A short-story deals with a single character, a single event, a single emotion, or the series of emotions called forth by a single situation." From Poe's attempt to define a *form* the short story quickly crystallized (some would say "ossified") into a *formula* that enjoyed enormous popularity with the public and popular-magazine editors at the turn of the century. Readers hungered for this quickly digested new fiction; hundreds of how-to books for writers in the early 1900s were based upon it. Indeed, it's influence can be seen most clearly in O. Henry's fiction, specifically his story of a classic reversal, "Gift of the Magi." It is present in the work of black America's first renowned short story writer, Charles Chesnutt (read "The Wife of His Youth"), in "The Monkey's Paw," and in many of Rod Serling's scripts for *The Twilight Zone*. In other words, so influential and powerful was this *form*-become-*formula* that for many twentieth-century readers it limned the contours of what a short story must *be*, and even today in novels, short stories, motion pictures, television episodes, and comic books instances of it provide the entertainment values of suspense, surprise, and intensity.

Inevitably, a backlash against the rigidity and predictability of this design had to occur. In his study on American literature, *The Symbolic Meaning*, D. H. Lawrence was at times savage in his criticism of the way Poe's "philosophy of composition" mechanized the form of the story to such an extent that life's mystery, spontaneity, and vitality were lost (these were crucial aesthetic aspects that defined Lawrence's own brilliant contribution to the novel and short story). In "Edgar Allan Poe," Lawrence decided that

> Poe is hardly an artist. He is rather a supreme scientist. . . .
> He is not sensual, he is sensational. The difference between
> these two is a difference between growth and decay. . . . As
> an artist Poe is unfailingly in bad taste—always bad taste.
> He seeks a sensation from every phrase or object and the
> effect is vulgar.

For Lawrence, "a tale is a concatenation of scientific cause and effect. But in a story the movement depends on the sudden appearance of spontaneous emotion or gesture, causeless, arising out of the living self." Most of those who rebelled in theory and practice damned the early-twentieth-century magazine editors for demanding that short fiction fit such an "artificial" mold. "The very technique of the short story is pathological," Herbert Ellsworth Cory stated in a 1917 article in *Dial*, "and titillates our nerves in our pathological moments. The short story is the blood kinsman of the quick-lunch, the vaudeville, and the joy-ride." Two years earlier, Henry Seidel Canby bemoaned in *The Atlantic Monthly:*

> Once started, the narrative must move, move, move furiously, each action and every speech pointing directly toward the unknown climax. A pause is a confession of weakness. . . . Then the climax, which must neatly, quickly, and definitely end the action for all time, either by a solution you have been urged to hope for by the wily author in every preceding paragraph, or in a way which is logically correct but never, never suspected.

For Canby, and many others, this "formula is rigid, not plastic as life is plastic. It fails to grasp innumerable stories which break the surface of American life day by day and disappear uncaught. Stories of quiet, homely life, events significant for themselves that never reach a burning climax, situations that end in irony, or doubt, or aspiration, it mars in the telling."

These judgments were shared by such fine storytellers as Sherwood Anderson. "As for the plot short stories of the magazines," he wrote in 1924, "those bastard children of de Maupassant, Poe, and O. Henry—it was certain there were no plot short stories ever lived in any life I had known anything about." In his own fiction in *Winesburg, Ohio*, Anderson rejected the earlier emphasis on plot-driven storytelling and focused on what he called a form that more organically "grew out of the materials of the tale and the teller's reaction to them."

We can say, in summary, that the early-nineteenth-century efforts to define the short story, which placed it on its feet as a distinct form, led quickly to senility, and that in turn produced an outcry for reform, specifically for greater artistic freedom, by the 1920s. This revolt against formalism was, of course, pervasive in all the arts after World War I—in poetry's free-verse movement, the paintings of Picasso, and the sculpture of Eric Gill. The Victorian era—and its vision of life—had ended. Just as a new science was beginning, signaled by the gathering of twenty-nine physicists to work on quantum mechanics in Brussels, Belgium, in 1927 (nine of the twenty-nine, among them Albert Einstein, later received Nobel Prizes for their contributions to quantum theory), so, too, were literary artists redefining their practice to create a distinctly twentieth-century literature.

Through the use of stream-of-consciousness techniques, James Joyce achieved a representation of subjective states of consciousness unequaled before or after *Ulysses* or *Finnegans*

Wake. Ernest Hemingway's devotion to craft produced a major style of writing, one so widely imitated that his influence is everywhere evident in the novelists of the 1950s, in all genres and subgenres, and clearly impacted the diction and word economy of "minimalist" storytellers (Raymond Carver) in the 1980s.

I agree with critic Alfred Kazin that Hemingway's subjects are emotionally adolescent (bullfights, hunting, and other violent activities), that he "brought a major art to a minor vision of life," but Hemingway's declaration of the writer's ambition shows he deeply understood how an individual artistic performance can significantly enhance culture. *Write what hasn't been written before or beat dead men at what they have done* helps us see that in at least one sense we can view the evolution of literature the same way we view the progress of science. At any given moment, physicists here and abroad are laboring to answer *objective* questions handed down by Einstein, Bohr, and others—tracking down subatomic entities, for example, or patching up cracks in Unified Field Theory; it's a competitive race of sorts, as James D. Watson points out in *The Double Helix*. Similarly, the history of literary practice creates objective aesthetic possibilities, artistic works demanded historically by the foul-ups and partial breakthroughs in past literary art, novels and stories that fill in the blanks and potholes created by the oversights and omissions of those writers who preceded us. No, these are not your average "commercial" novels or mere entertainments, only great books that advance literary practice. As the old saying goes, good fiction sharpens our perception; great fiction *changes* it.

In the realm of American literature at *any* time there are *always* subjects, unexplored, that cry out for dramatization—for example, until 1998 no novel philosophically treated the life of Martin Luther King Jr. until my own *Dreamer* appeared; and I would submit that today's literary fiction has yet to broach either the complexity and meaning of the scientific discoveries I briefly cataloged at the beginning of this essay, or the remarkable multicultural texture of the American social world in the late 1990s.

Or beat dead men at what they have done. Again, Hemingway illuminates how each significant advance in writing need not involve a new subject. Rather, it is quite enough if that work completes or expands upon an earlier, flawed performance, or deepens its investigations as Ellison's many-splendored *Invisible Man* opens the subject of black American life in the 1940s to greater imaginative realms than Wright achieved in *Native Son.* Ellison's book does *not* "refute" Wright's novel. Both works are masterpieces—one of naturalism, the other of surrealism and sumptuous stylistic synthesis. But, yes, *Invisible Man,* in its multileveled philosophical explorations, embodied a far greater vision and wider deployment of *techne* than *Native Son,* the work of Ellison's mentor.

Can we speak of literary "progress" in other ways? I believe we can. When Western audiences became better informed about the world through the mediums of radio and newscasts and later television, fiction put aside its nineteenth-century burden of *reportage.* While there are readers today who apparently enjoy this (I know of one professor at Boston University who argued one night over dinner that what makes Melville's *Moby-Dick* a great novel is the fact that one can learn about whaling from it), contemporary writers can leave travelogue material to the travel writers, concentrating instead on creating economical, poetic, descriptive passages in which each and every image reinforces character, atmosphere, tone, and event. We can also say that characterization in twentieth-century fiction advances beyond much of what appeared in nineteenth-century literature, where too often characters were defined one-dimensionally by a single, dominant emotion or trait (nobility, envy, love) and thereby left much to be desired in terms of human complexity, as in Harriet Beecher Stowe's *Uncle Tom's Cabin*. Except in mass-market pulp writing, what author Fred Pfeil once called "industrial fiction," or in B movies, melodrama has disappeared—at least where serious, literary fiction is concerned.

Also left behind with the nineteenth century are *sentimentality* and *purple prose*. Oh yes, Harlequin romances, so popular today, are steeped in both, and their readers consume (or so I've been told by one writer for this subgenre) three such novels a day on average; they are popular largely with women readers who want the same love story told over and over, with variations only in setting and time. But this, obviously, is not art. For the finest literary fiction of the twentieth century is, if nothing else, so acutely aware of language performance—consider the work of Nabokov, Djuna Barnes in *Nightwood*, or William Gass's novels—that this cliché-larded, mawkish sentence from Mary J. Holmes's justifiably forgotten novel *Madeline* (1881) could never appear on the pages of a serious fiction in 2000 C.E.: "He bent down over her now, for her face was hidden in her hands, all sense of sight shut out, all sense of hearing, too, save the words he was pouring into her ear—words which burned their way into her heart, making it throb for a single moment with gratified pride, and then grow heavy as lead as she knew how impossible it was for her to pay the debt in the way which he wanted."

Progress, indeed.

Except for the enduring masterpieces of earlier times, contemporary writing in general is *better* in respect to craft—and on the level of the sentence—than garden-variety prose fiction of the nineteenth century. In their forms, the novel and short story are creatively freer, and this liberation can be traced not only to the innovators of the 1920s but also to the so-called imaginative writers of the "New Fiction" (and "magical realism") that emerged in the 1970s, authors such as John Gardner, Robert Coover, and John Barth, who deserve credit for developing fresh strategies for solving the problems of viewpoint, opening our fiction to exciting new (and sometimes old) ontologies, and for unsealing a door to "fabulation" closed since the nineteenth century by the hard-core naturalists. Inside that room of fictional possibilities they found a tale- and yarn-telling tradition still close to the roots of oral storytelling, where one could discover philosophical insights in fairy tales, folklore, and myths: stories about fantastic creatures—golems and grendels—we are not likely to bump into at the corner supermarket, but in the New Fiction we could. For in the universe of the mind (and the college-based New Fiction writers were interested in nothing if not mind, perception, epistemology), Frankenstein's monster and JFK, quarks and Pegasus, Rip Van Winkle and Chairman Mao all existed side by side as phenomenal objects for consciousness, none more "real" than another in our dreams or between the covers of a book. It is a fiction conscious of itself *as* fiction, and conscious of storytelling's four-millennia-old traditions. Indeed, in a post-Wittgenstein-and-Heidegger period, in a postmodern culture aware of a subatomic world of protons and electrons in constant motion unknown to the nineteenth century, some of the New Fiction's authors presented "reality" itself as a cultural construct, an interpretation of experience, a *fiction* based on the ensorcelling power of language alone.

To these changes we must add one final instance of progress that is of enormous importance. Since the 1970s, writers of color—who for centuries were marginalized or simply ignored— have irreversibly transformed the social world as it is portrayed in American fiction. Moreover, their stories depicting black, Asian, Native American, and Hispanic experiences and history have broadened as well as deepened the way we perceive ourselves and this nation's past. In the hands of bestselling and award-winning writers such as Richard Wright, Ralph Ellison, Maxine Hong Kingston, Oscar Hijuelos, Toni Morrison, Amy Tan, Ha Jin, Leslie Silko, and Jhumpa Lahiri, the novel and short story *opened* for late-twentieth-century readers onto lives, events, and nonwhite views of the world that qualified and refined the fictional practice of former times by making readers conscious—sometimes painfully so—of the racial and cultural Others whose presence in America and the world is as essential and worthy of study as the lives of northern Europeans.

Many have claimed that literature is dangerous. They are right to fear its power. The list of novels banned from high school English classes in the twentieth century reads like a roster of the most lauded modern and contemporary fiction. The reason for this, I believe, is twofold. First, because fiction at its best challenges the status quo. It forces us to question our social relations, prejudices, understanding of the world, ourselves, and the meaning of humanity. It can be scientifically prescient, anticipating the impact of technology—and even specific inventions—on our lives, an event that happens frequently in first-rate science fiction. It can fuel civil war, as Stowe's *Uncle Tom's Cabin* did in the nineteenth century; expose political systems, as George Orwell did with *1984* and *Animal Farm;* lead to reforms in the way patients are treated in mental institutions, which occurred after Ken Kesey published *One Flew Over the Cuckoo's Nest;* and inspire resistance to oppression, as Winston Churchill discovered when he read "If We Must Die," a poem by Harlem Renaissance writer Claude McKay, over the airwaves during the Nazi bombing of London.

Secondly, literature is dangerous *ontologically* because reading is the most radical and liberating of all enterprises. (Thus, novels are banned, and in the antebellum South it was illegal to teach slaves how to read.) Open any novel. What is there? Black marks—signs—on white paper. First they are silent. They are lifeless, lacking signification until the consciousness of the reader imbues them with meaning, allowing a fictitious character like Huckleberry Finn, say, to emerge hugely from the monotonous rows of ebony type. Once this magical act takes place in the mind of the reader, an entire world appears redivivus, in his consciousness: "a vivid and continuous dream," as John Gardner once called it, one that so ensorcells us that we forget the room we're sitting in or fail to hear the telephone ring. In other words, the world experienced within any book is *transcendent*. It exists for consciousness alone (Huckleberry Finn exists *only* as a mental construct, like a mathematical entity). But, as Jean-Paul Sartre describes so well in his classic work *What Is Literature?* the rare experience found in books is the "conjoint effort of author and reader." It is dialectical. While the writer composes his "world" in words, his (or her) work requires an attentive reader who will "put himself from the very beginning and almost without a guide at the height of this silence" of signs. Reading, Sartre tells us, is *directed creation*. A contract of sorts. "To write is to make an appeal to the reader that he lead into objective existence the revelation which I have undertaken by means of language." Do you get it? I hope so. For each book *requires* that a reader exercise his orbific freedom for the "world" and theater of meaning embodied on its pages to *be*. As readers, we invest the cold signs on the pages of *Native Son* with our *own* emotions, *our* understanding of poverty, oppression, and fear; then, in what is almost an act of thaumaturgy, the powerful figures and tropes Wright has created reward us richly by returning our subjective feelings to us transformed, refined, and alchemized by language into a new vision with the capacity to change our lives forever.

This magic rests in your hands, as readers. It is a power to co-create and travel through numerous imaginative and intellectual realms that one can invoke at any time, anywhere. A power that serves democracy itself. If film is a communal experience, as so many have claimed, then reading is the triumph of the individual consciousness and human freedom.

However, that freedom we experience in literature is frequently won at a great expense by fiction's creators. Nonwhite writers, and the innovators who advanced the novel and story as disciplines, often had to publish outside the "mainstream" of American literature at the beginning of their careers. Many black authors found acceptance for their creations only in black publications before placing their work with white publishing companies. It is well known that in the 1920s, a revolutionary period for Western literature, many authors found their break with the status quo forced them into self-publishing. Or some received recognition first in Europe before their art was lauded at home. Closer to our own time, "experimental" writers originally rejected by New York publishers—Ronald Sukenick, Jonathan Baumbach, Russell Banks, and Clarence Major—founded the Fiction Collective, a publishing cooperative controlled by writers themselves, to insure that their unusual and daring ways of telling stories reached the public. It is a fact that American culture at any time has been dominated by commercial fiction, which seldom, if ever, innovates in the ways Hemingway called for. Thus, in order for their works to see the light of day, our artists of vision have relied upon small presses and numerous literary journals, most of which are too poor to pay contributors or reward them well. Yet it is there that many of tomorrow's most important authors are publishing their stories and novel excerpts.

If we hope to see the continued formal and thematic growth of American literature in this century, it is incumbent upon the

public to financially support those small presses and "little magazines" that allow unknown and iconoclastic writers to break into
print. For twenty years I have insisted upon this with my own
writing students, graduate and undergraduate. Each term I ask
them to subscribe to a literary journal of distinction they would
·like their work to appear in, to *read* that publication for a year,
and by doing so support other artists in their community. This is
but a small gesture we all, as individual citizens concerned about
literary art, can perform.

But more than small gestures are required. Since the late
1960s, the National Endowment for the Arts has each year given
individual fellowships to American writers, invariably young
creators of talent, whose selection is made by a panel of accom-
plished writers who review thousands of submissions. The
grants, I believe, are now at $20,000 each. They buy crucial
writing time for "emerging" talents, who must maintain fatigu-
ing "day jobs" in order to support their art. Unfortunately, the
NEA has in recent years been a lightning rod for controversy,
specifically for projects it funded in the areas of performance
and plastic arts, not literature, that offended the values of conservative Americans. Time and again our elected officials in the
House of Representatives have called for the abolition of supporting the arts through the national treasury. The market, they
argue, should determine what art succeeds and what art fails—
the public, in other words, should be allowed to support a performance or simply walk away.

This argument is not without merit, but its proponents fail to
recognize that if the public—the market—at any moment is chosen as the sole arbiter of which artistic works will be supported,
ephemeral fashions and social whims will replace critical standards. By this standard, we would have lost long ago groundbreaking novels and stories that were misunderstood in their

time, or were decades ahead of their time, but now are canonized. Any nation that genuinely cares about the health of its cultural life must politically support those in Congress devoted to funding the NEA, which in addition to issuing grants to individual writers also funds a wide range of literary journals that could not survive without its annual support.

All art entertains; but all entertainment is *not* art. Any nation that understands the difference between these two—art as escapist fare and art as enduring cultural artifact—will support literature's efflorescence, even as it must fund research and development in the sciences. And, lastly, it must see the wisdom in Nobel laureate Saul Bellow's observation in his 1970s essay "Culture Now":

> This society, like decadent Rome, is an amusement society. Art cannot and should not compete with amusement. It has business at the heart of humanity. The artist, as Collingwood tells us, must be a prophet, "not in the sense that he foretells things to come, but that he tells the audience, at the risk of their displeasure, the secrets of their own hearts." That is why he exists. He is a spokesman for his community. This account of the artist's business is old, much older than Collingwood, very old, but in modern times this truth, which we all feel, is seldom expressed. No community altogether knows its own heart, and by failing in this knowledge a community deceives itself on the one subject concerning which ignorance means death. The remedy is art itself. Art is the community's medicine for the worst disease of mind, the corruption of consciousness.

The Beginner's Mind

To be perfectly honest with you, I don't know what a writer should be. And I always wince when I call myself a writer, despite the fact that I've been publishing stories since I was seventeen. My formal training was not in a writing program, although I've taught now for twenty-six years at the University of Washington alongside splendid colleagues such as David Wagoner, the late Nelson Bentley and William Matthews, Heather McHugh, Sharon Bryan, Shawn Wong, Colleen McElroy, Maya Sonenberg, David Bosworth, and David Shields. They are real writers to me, and when I'm in their company, I sometimes feel like a fraud.

I feel that way because when I was a teenager, my great and only passion was to be a professional cartoonist, which I was for seven terrific years. Then, when I was in my late teens, philosophy became my second passion, and I received my doctorate in that field. I came to writing not because I wanted to be a writer but because when I was twenty-two years old the idea for a philosophical novel came to me and would not leave me alone. I couldn't sleep at night for thinking about the characters and their possibilities. So I wrote that book over the summer of 1970, and it was predictably awful.

But I did learn from that experience how to organize 250 pages of something, which I'd never done before. And I found the experience—the process of discovery—to be as seductive and rewarding as the work I was doing in philosophy. So I wrote another book. Then a third one.

And a fourth. At the end of two years, I had six. I was so thrilled by the process I trained myself to write ten pages a day. All six of those novels went through three drafts. Because I wasn't in a writing program, I didn't have anyone to tell me that what I was doing was outrageous. The school I attended used the quarter system. I was used to taking a class and finishing it within ten weeks. And I didn't see any reason why you couldn't do that with a novel. So I did, one book a quarter for two years until I started the seventh book and decided maybe I needed some help.

Maintaining Discipline and a Beginner's Mind

Help arrived in the incredible person of the late John Gardner, who was then a young professor in the English Department at Southern Illinois University. Most of you know something about Gardner's work, but I would like to testify that, as his former student, he provided me with an astonishing example of what an artist and scholar could be. Gardner knew twelve languages, ancient and modern. He was a Chaucer scholar. Gardner so loved the poet Homer that at age forty-five he taught himself

Greek in order to do his own translation of *The Iliad* for his students, whose work Gardner published at his own expense in a magazine he started in the 1950s. He translated Japanese authors whose work he admired and published twenty-seven of his own books—novels, literary criticism, short stories, and poetry.

He wrote librettos, screenplays, book reviews, everything possible in the English language, and on top of all that he played the French horn. In short, Gardner was a writer—a teacher of writing—on whom nothing of importance in the world around him (or the literature of the past) was lost. Since he was the first "serious," literary writer I met, I just assumed his indefatigable energy, passion, love of great storytelling, originality, and productivity were characteristics that he expected all his apprentice writers to develop.

With him looking over my shoulder, I wrote my seventh book, *Faith and the Good Thing*, in nine months, which I—at age twenty-four—thought was a terribly long period to devote to a novel or to anything else. Gardner brought me into the book world, where I was a complete innocent, although I had published two books of drawings and created an early PBS how-to-draw series before I met Gardner. But I was an artistic Grendel among the literary Danes. I didn't know the subculture of "serious" writers, or why—as Gardner's friend and literary executor Nicholas Delbanco once put it—they all talked in a kind of clipped, elliptical shorthand, which I'm still working to perfect.

I was tabula rasa, without any rigid preconceptions about literature, what it should be, or how writers should think or behave, or what were appropriate or inappropriate subjects to explore. In fact, as a phenomenologist—that was my orientation in philosophy—I was inclined to "bracket" or set aside all assumptions about the world (or as many as I could) whenever I examined phenomena. To this day, when I sit down to write a story, I don't ask myself what a story is or what the rules should be; I just try to listen to the characters, try to see clearly and vividly what they're going to do next, and chase down any thought, any image, or any impression that arises during the creative process, even if it contradicts my most cherished ideas and beliefs.

With each new story or novel or essay or screenplay or item of literary criticism, I've always returned to what Buddhists call beginner's mind. Each new story shows me what a story can be. All my early models were from philosophy—where authors like George Santayana, Miguel de Unamuno, Jean-Paul Sartre, and William Gass worked on fiction one day, then wrestled with an essay on epistemology the next. I never developed the ability to perform a kind of apartheid on creativity; I never learned how to segregate my interests in fiction, philosophy, history, the visual arts, and the martial arts because they all struck me as forms of expression, means for interpretation, and ways of getting at the truth.

And I'll reveal to you something even stranger.

What Should One Write About?

When I first began writing, I was never interested in writing about myself. I saw my own daily life as pretty ordinary and boring and predictable, and I still like it that way. I much preferred to tell imaginative stories. In fact, rather than dwell on myself in my writing, I was more fascinated and intrigued, for example, by the dilemma of Descartes when I read the following in a book by Bertrand Russell.

In 1649, Queen Christina of Sweden became interested in Descartes' work, and prevailed upon him to come to

Stockholm. This Scandinavian sovereign was a true renaissance character. Strong-willed and vigorous, she insisted that Descartes should teach her philosophy at five in the morning. This unphilosophic hour of rising at dead of night in a Swedish winter was more than Descartes could endure. He took ill and died in February 1650.

Rather than autobiography or memoir, it was a tale such as Descartes's that sparked my imagination. And I was powerfully intrigued by the real-life stories I heard in the black world, stories about the ex-cowboy Charlie Smith who at 137 years old was the oldest living American in 1978, stories about the struggles of the young Booker T. Washington, or stories about how the all-black town of Allensworth was founded in California around the turn of the century. When I was young, these stories never appeared in my high school and college textbooks, and they were not in our fiction any more than the life and legacy of Martin Luther King Jr. has been explored in our imaginative literature.

THE WRITER AS MIDWIFE

So, naturally, when I began to teach at the University of Washington in 1976, I was hopeful that perhaps my students would turn in stories that filled in the gaps in our cultural and intellectual history. I'm very happy to report that one of my former students from the late 1970s, David Guterson, did just that with his award-winning novel, *Snow Falling on Cedars*, which by now has probably sold over a billion copies. I watched him from the time he was twenty years old. He was dedicated. He was determined to write well and not about himself. He would take pages of a story he was working on, paste them into a college notebook, then carry that notebook around so he could revise his fiction all day long as he rode the bus to work or went to the baseball game of one of his children. And if you've read *Snow Falling on Cedars*, or if you've seen the movie, you'll know this book is not about Guterson. Rather, it is a gift. It is the lives of Japanese-Americans in the Northwest that he is writing about. He is simply the midwife for their story. And when a midwife is finished delivering a beautiful baby, the last thing she does is jump in front of the baby and wave her hands and shout, "Look what *I* did!" No, the midwife gets out of the way and moves on to the next delivery and the next and the next.

By the way, Guterson stopped by my house in Seattle the day after Christmas a few years ago. He came to pick up the present I had set aside for him. And when he went back to his car, he opened the trunk and showed me the research materials he'd picked up earlier that day at the University of Washington library for the new novel he was working on. He had lots of books. I saw a dissertation on the state of nursing in the 1940s, and he was very excited about the process of discovery he found himself in with the characters, their "world," and the themes in his new novel. Indeed, the process is the alpha and omega for Guterson.

Unfortunately, the vast majority of my former students at UW during the last two decades were not like Dave Guterson. Most of them would probably agree with what one intermediate short story writing student told me in the mid-1980s. I had just finished lecturing on some aspect of fiction and I gave my students a photocopy of what I call "A Theory for This Course," printed here in its entirety. Please don't laugh as you read it. I was a much younger, fire-breathing professor on his first teaching job and eager to take on the world when I wrote these words.

Real writers—journeymen writers—are technicians. They do not cringe fearfully before a creative writing chore, but regard it with healthy contempt. It is merely a task and, as technicians, the real writers know that they have at their disposal several ways of executing it successfully.

If you are a writer who regards literary creation as, not merely a possible profession, but as a passion, there is always something to do. If you are not writing fresh material, you are revising; if you are not revising, you are reading—literature, philosophy, mythology, the sciences—everything that employs the word. If you're not researching, you are relaxing over a meal, or with a book, or a film, but only truly with a portion of your mind—the rest of your thoughts are mindful of how the film or book is constructed, and even at the dinner table (yes, even here) as you sip a glass of wine (if you drink wine) you are—or should be—focusing on the particular taste, smell, and feel of things so you won't draw a blank when you sit down at the typewriter. [The word *typewriter* tells you how old this document is.] And so a first principle emerges for your writing: observe. It is the world itself that is your subject. Not necessarily an objective, pre-established world where meaning has been worked out, but one that requires your voice and vision to make it more intelligible.

It is incumbent upon the creative writer to find, cultivate, and sustain his or her own individual voice and vision, and this is the project of a lifetime. Regardless of the work and sacrifice, regardless of the years of apprenticeship required, there is no other goal worthy of an apprentice writer. You must learn the craft of your predecessors thoroughly and, when the happy moment comes, contribute your own work in such a way that it is continuous with the past of your discipline yet projects into the future. If these goals sound lofty, they are meant to be because we live at a time when the competition for publication is severe. Therefore, it is crucial that your fictions should be complete in every respect. For this course, they must present (1) a story with logically plotted sequences; (2) three-dimensional characters, that is, real people with real problems; (3) sensuous description, or a complete "world" to which the senses of the reader can imaginatively respond; (4) dialogue with the authenticity of real speech; (5) a strong narrative voice; (6) rhythm, musicality, and control of the cadences in your fiction; (7) and, finally, originality in theme and execution. Lacking these elements, there is surely no reason why readers, who are already tightfisted about their time, should spend half an hour with your story when they could be playing with their children, working out, or enjoying an evening with friends.

And that brings me to the heart of this essay, the single point that underlies the endless study of craft, why one creates fiction in the first place instead of, say, selling dictionaries from door to door, and how such work—constant writing and rewriting—is bearable. The writer is not a leader. He or she is not, as some nineteenth-century poets may have believed, always the best seer. The writer, when he is most authentic, is a servant who, seeing what others perhaps have missed, gently and persuasively informs them of a meaning by making them feel its presence in the theater of a fiction. Such an author writes about people for people, and it is surely a fact that no writer should put on paper anything he or she could not say to someone's face.

After I was finished huffing and puffing, a young woman sitting in the classroom raised her hand, and she said, "You know,

I'm glad you told us that." I asked her why. She said, "Because now I understand that I don't want to be a great writer. I just want to write a few stories and maybe get some of them published, and that's all."

And I said, "Okay. That is fair. I will do everything possible to help you reach that goal," and I did. I would say after teaching thousands of young writers in workshops that 98 percent of my students enroll for precisely the reasons this young woman did. No doubt they do learn to be better readers of fiction. And some of them will go on to publish well, like my former student Gary Hawkes (a contemporary of Guterson), who is now chair of the English Department at Lycoming College and had two novels, *Semaphore* and *Surveyor,* published simultaneously in the summer of 1998. What I'm saying is that much of my job is to serve young writers who have strictly commercial ambitions or simply want to tell stories about their first sexual experiences.

THAT SAME PROF'S ADVICE
TWENTY YEARS LATER

However, my mission here is to reiterate the obvious, and with all humility, by saying that if writing teachers do not present students with the finest literary work from the past and present as models for the future, models that they draw from all disciplines—history, painting, biography, philosophy, the sciences, the cultures of the so-called Third World—they will not produce the David Gutersons of tomorrow. Our best teachers teach students how to write in numerous forms, Western and Eastern, because these forms are their global inheritance. Good teachers make you think about why James Alan McPherson says, whenever he writes a story, he feels the duty, the moral obligation, to

include some datum of black American history—which is
American history—in that story because the lives of people of
color, who shaped this country's evolution from the year 1619,
have been marginalized and are hardly known. Good teachers
tell you that if you want to be a good midwife, and not just a nar-
cissistic writer, you must devote a lifetime to craft. And after
saying that, they tell you what Gichin Funakoshi, the founder of
Goju-Ryu karate, said about the martial arts also works for writing: spirit *first*, technique second. (Then they tell you it's okay to
sometimes contradict yourself, as I just did.)

Good teachers convey to students the thoughts of Ernest
Hemingway, who said, "What a writer in our time has to do is
write what hasn't been written or beat dead men at what they
have done." They tell you it takes fifteen years for a fiction
writer to become "established" after he or she first publishes.
They tell you that you must master all the exercises at the end
of John Gardner's *The Art of Fiction*, as I urged David Guterson
and Gary Hawkes to do. They tell you that you must be inter-
disciplinary, be able to solve any writing problem three different
ways, and find the perfect painting, sculpture, and piece of
music or work of philosophy that complements your fiction.
They tell you that you must be prolific as a writer, if only to survive, and especially prolific if you are a black, brown, or Asian
writer. They tell you to research a literary form not used for a
major work in the last hundred years—some literary dinosaur
once popular in the West or the East, then pushed aside by the
course of fiction's evolution—and then have you plot a new
story using its conventions, updating them for a late-twentieth-
century audience as I did in my second novel, *Oxherding Tale*.
They tell you that writing well is the same damned thing as
thinking well. Not just being clever, but thinking critically and
independently.

The Four Rules

And, finally, to shore up their students for the lifelong creative adventures that await them, good teachers recite August Wilson's four rules of playwriting. These, of course, apply to all creative work. Wilson's Rules for Writing are as follows:

1. There are no rules.
2. The first rule is wrong, so pay attention.
3. You can't write for an audience; the writer's first job is to survive.
4. You can make no mistakes, but anything you write can be made better.

Exercises

1. Make an exhaustive list of historical events or figures who have long intrigued you.
2. Choose five from the above list and write for five minutes on each of them, exploring their metaphorical possibilities in a work of fiction.
3. Do some research and then write a short story that centers in full or in part on one of the events or figures.

A Phenomenology of
On Moral Fiction

I

In his first book, an anthology called *The Forms of Fiction* (1962),
John Gardner offered an opinion that sixteen years later, and
after only slight revision, became the major premise for *On
Moral Fiction:* "A good writer," he says, "must believe that individual human beings are important, that they have free will, and
that they are (regardless of whether or not the writer believes in
God) at least metaphorically created in the image of God and, at
least potentially, only a little lower than the angels" (page 17).
Aesthetics has always been the scandal of philosophy, the bastard
child who, despite our best theories, remains in the realm of
opinion and prejudice. If *On Moral Fiction* fails as real philosophy, as nearly every critic claims, it is partly because the subject
itself defies objective treatment. In order to examine the "truth"
of such subjective realms as the religious, ethical, psychic, racial,

and aesthetic, a descriptive analysis is required; but to my knowledge, no reviewer (or artist) has looked seriously at Gardner's thesis strictly from the standpoint of experience and meaning. So far our critics have, like Aristotle's bad critics in *The Poetics,* reacted irresponsibly, rejecting the problem of "moral fiction" ("responsible fiction" may be a better phrase, but not half as sexy) and Gardner for reasons that have nothing whatsoever to do with literary aesthetics, or accepting it because Gardner has said, as it were, what some of them already believed. The only genuine response is to think *along* with the author, grasp his intentions, and, if possible, build upon his firmer insights.

Criticism, of course, cannot separate a writer's life from his products. In every artist's work we witness the same questions raised from book to book as he circles back, year in year out, to a single problem. For Gardner, the meditation from *The Forms of Fiction* through *Mickelsson's Ghosts* was the problem of affirming values we wish to believe after the overly discussed disintegration of the traditional (and objective) order. If his fictions and essays seem, in the final analysis, unabashedly Protestant, and anchored in a (white) Middle American Lifeworld that died (some say) with the family farm, it is because Gardner (who was not naive about cities and nonwhite people) was never seduced by postmodernism. Not the trendy experiments in fragmentation and arbitrariness as novelty, nor the critic's fascination with displacement, nihilism, and discontinuity. He did, in fact, believe (uneasily, like any modern artist) in the truth of Christianity, or at least viewed its fundamental notions of sacrifice, love, and service as unbeatable ideals;[1] he was probably one of the last American novelists to acknowledge the racial and political horrors of our history, yet wrote as if he truly believed in the decency of American democracy,[2] the Republican Party, and in the literary standards (and methods) established by Homer,

Chaucer, and Shakespeare—standards that required him to compose in every form we've inherited, and invent a few new ones by a technique he calls "genre-crossing." In other words, the strange *problematic* of this man and his work, the "project" that animated his nearly thirty books was: How can one convincingly dramatize the values of our predecessors and what they have left us when, as everyone knows, modern man has killed the magic in everything? What most characterizes this queer age we inhabit is the fact that everything from the earth to the old gods (values) has been transformed (since Descartes) into an object for the *ego cogito*, devalued, reduced to our I-ness, swallowed up in subjectivity. God is *our* value. We have slain—as Nietzsche proclaimed more in shock than celebration—everything that *is* in itself. The world of shared values is splintered into billions of perspectives, each as "true" as any other. Sadly, each man today is his own lawgiver; he breathes air spoiled by the Freudian assault on reason, the Vienna Circle's sneering denial of beliefs empirically undemonstrable (God, beauty, the Good), and pop existentialism's adolescent idea of freedom as self-gratification. It is this false individualism and falling away from reason and righteousness that Gardner so railed against in literature and life—a form of self-consciousness, solipsism, and (what is the same thing) selfishness. In his novels and short fiction he was fighting mad about it, especially in *Grendel* and "The Warden," but he often failed, it's true, to be entirely convincing.

To invoke the simple experience of love and life affirmation Gardner sometimes relied on dazzling imitation (itself an act of love), or used the sensational techniques he so disliked in "toy fiction," though he used them better than most "experimental" writers: Barthean intrusion ("The King's Indian"), and stories often fueled by their own proliferating mechanisms rather than reality (but isn't this exactly the point at issue: reality?). These slips into postmodernism were, perhaps, a gifted writer's back-handed concession to readers reared on the antinovel and surfiction, but the techniques—what they say—may be at war with Gardner's belief in "the holiness of things,"[3] the belief that things are not reducible to reflective consciousness—or, if they are, that their value is greater, not less. His most successful strategy (in my opinion) has been the appropriation of old forms such as the architechtonic novel (*Sunlight Dialogues*), fairy tales ("King of the Hummingbirds"), fables ("Trumpeter"), pastorals, and the epic (*Jason and Medeia*), because these vehicles are so rich that, by virtue of their having been in circulation for centuries, new fictions in these forms have the authority lacking in so much "interior" modern literature. Meaning *accumulates* in the form, infuses these fictions with dignity, affirmation, and a timeless sense of value, which possibly confused readers used to cynicism and, I suspect, accounts for much of the knee-jerk criticism Gardner has received. Regardless, he was our most inventive, prolific, and controversial writer of serious fiction. He is the only writer today whose fictions offer us the achievements of the past—artistic and metaphysical—as models for the future.

Unfortunately, Gardner's ideas on art cannot be systematically argued, at least not in my view. And they are threatened on two sides: by philosophers who will dismiss them as unclear, and by writers who feel their freedom is in danger. His discussion of the spiritual crisis in Dante and Sartre is ingenious, his public scrap with William Gass on the nature of words an important, friendly feud that concretely relates the major philosophical problem of our time—language—to literary practice, but his essay, despite its energy and the power of Gardner's prose, too often fails to clearly define its crucial terms. It vastly oversimplifies (as Gardner knew and said in his later interviews) the complex relation between society and art, consciousness and language, art and madness; leaves valuable insights on the theory of art as process dangling; leaps prematurely from one proposition to the next in order to push on; is repetitive; and dismisses nearly every American writer today as mediocre, which may be true, but he forgets his own advice that a critic must show compassion and sympathy. Yet, having admitted all this, I must add that *On Moral Fiction*'s methodological dilemmas are more interesting (and influential) than the tightest arguments in most journals of aesthetics, and that many of us secretly wish we had written this provocative book. Like Sartre's *What Is Literature?* and Collingwood's *The Principles of Art* (both flawed but beautiful works), it gives both readers and writers the opportunity to ask, in the grand sense, "What does fiction *do*?" More importantly, we're forced to ask, "What *should* it do?" These are the problems I wish to discuss—first the relation between nature and thought (fiction), because we can't talk ethics before we talk metaphysics, then the sticky question of "morality" as it relates to the problem of interpretation.

II

Under close inspection, the so-called modern dilemmas of subjectivism and the breakdown of objective standards are not so modern after all. As Gardner knew, and shows in *The Wreckage of Agathon*, Western philosophy is born out of this perennial debate on the nature of meaning. The pre-Socratic philosophers faced it in the form of Protagorean teachings to the effect that perceptual experience, what things *mean*, differs from subject to subject. If this is so—if meaning is perspectival, shifting such that all races, individuals, and historical subjects have their own truth—then they must also have their own distinct values, which no appeal to a pre-established "reality" can affirm or deny. Nature arbitrates nothing. Insofar as facts exist at all in nature, they carry an ensemble of meanings. Everyone is wrong. Everyone is right. In this case, it is bad form to even ask what is moral. The liberal-humanist tradition embraces this belief in the multiplicity of truths, this polymorphous side of perception—as does phenomenology—but the built-in danger is that it leads, often, to what Gardner calls "pseudomorality" (delight in the most bizarre perspective, like that of Jean Genet, as *the* truth) and the destruction of a *shared* world of standards to bind us to the things we love. Plato, to resolve this, proposed a perfect, Parmenidian realm of meaning in which we "participated" imperfectly; Hegel (who was not always wrong) suggested the world was *becoming* truthful as we argued about it, and that the totality of our perspectives delivered the Whole, which remained a mystery until the end of history, or until (maybe) we won a seat in heaven; and Edmund Husserl, a mathematician-philosopher, who read little Hegel but hated the consequences of ambiguity, settled on the somewhat shaky concept of "empathy" (*Einfühlung*) to bridge subjectivities. Gardner, too, finds empathy to be a link between subjects, Leibnizian monads, when he discusses "character" as the most important element in fiction.

To write well, for Gardner, is to obliterate for the duration of your fiction your own pettiness, to surrender *your* prejudices in order to seize another man's way of seeing—his truth, the way the world appears to *him*, then faithfully present it in the story. In this way he modifies Aristotle's notion of *mimesis:* "Would *she* lift the coffee cup?"[4] (For classic mimesis to work, we must first agree on what *is* before it can be imitated; since we are in strong disagreement on the Real, and have abandoned the idea that nature's meaning is pregiven, the artist is obliged, then, to reconstruct as best he can perspectives on the Real.) When he calls the *process* of fiction "moral," it is because we, as writers, do believe in the interchangeability of standpoints and find it necessary to transport ourselves *over there* into a body inhabited by someone else (every "over there" is potentially a "here" for us), adopting, as he does for James Page in *October Light,* the book where Gardner truly excels at characterization, the limitations and weaknesses of someone we care enough about to fictionalize, particularly at the moment he faces an incident that challenges his beliefs. Some may see this as no more than an exercise in the imagination—Gardner's "What Kind of Smoke Are You?" game—but it is philosophically sound. It is a fundamental axiom of the social world that "If I were there, where he is now, then I would experience things in the same perspective, distance, and reach as he does. And, if he were here where I am, he would experience things from the same perspective as I."[5] We throw ourselves *with* a character toward his projects, divest ourselves of our own historically acquired peculiarities, and reconstruct his world.[6] This is difficult. This is dangerous, for what the author believed before starting his story—the point he wanted to make—will, in all likelihood, be severely modified. (But isn't this exactly the process of truth?) Since we write fiction, not essays or autobiography disguised as fiction, this process is often most interesting when men explore the meaning (being) of phenomena from the viewpoint of women; when blacks write about whites, and whites about blacks. But you are saying, "It is *arrogant* for a white writer to think he can adopt a black point of view!" We see the Other's eyes, but we cannot see *through* his eyes. Because one consequence of the breakdown in standards is the belief that we *can't* have someone else's toothache, or know her well enough to decide if she'd lift the cup, it is necessary to say one more thing about the relativity of truth and our differing "subjective worlds."

Empathy is a fine moral idea, as far as it goes, but it does not say what we all have to admit, sooner or later, about truth's variation among subjects. If you go deeply enough into relativity, you encounter the transcendence of relativism; in philosopher Maurice Merleau-Ponty's terms, "to retire into oneself is to leave oneself."[7] Why is this so? Because what we have are, not different worlds, but instead innumerable perspectives on *one* world; and we know that when it comes to the crunch, we share, all of us, the same cultural Lifeworld—a world layered with ancestors, predecessors, and contemporaries. To think this world properly is to find that all our perspectives take us directly to a common situation, a common history in which all meanings evolve.[8] Merleau-Ponty writes in *Adventures of the Dialectic:*

> My own field of thought and action is made up of imperfect meanings, badly defined and interrupted. They are completed over there, in the others who hold the key to them because they see sides of things that I do not see, as well as, one might say, my social back. Likewise, I am the only one capable of tallying the balance sheets of their lives, for their meanings are also incomplete and are openings onto something that I alone am able to see. I do not have to search very far for the others: I find them in my experience, lodged in the hollows that show what they see and what I fail to see. Our experiences thus have lateral relationships of truth: all together, each possessing clearly what is secret to the other, in our combined functionings we form a totality which moves toward enlightenment and completion. . . . We are never locked in ourselves.[9]

Fiction, truly responsible storytelling, is, therefore, a *we* relation. It exhibits this richness of sense; it strives for interpretative *completeness* as the writer (like an actor) adopts the role and real place of each character. A "moral fiction," then, may do no more than rotate around various perspectives, treating each truth as if it were *the* truth (which it is for a character) and settle on no position at all. Showing us different, new ways of seeing may, after all, be enough for a work of art—it is certainly true to experience, insofar as it shows meaning to be historical, evolving, changing; but I think John Gardner was asking for more than this.

Even if each interpretation has its integrity, is it possible that some are, so to speak, more equal (or better) than others? Now we step into deeper waters. If you enjoy Dickens, while I enjoy Ed Bullins, there is little trouble—we will fight for each man's right to his own viewpoint; but if you tell me we should all write like an Englishman who seems as comfortable in the world as in his living room, then I shall feel there is something wrong with you. Or, putting this another way, a Thrasymachus (or Robert Ringer) turns to nature and is rewarded by the perception that self-interest is the dominant sense of things—he teaches us, I suppose, *a* truth, but should we give the man a chorus? Gardner's answer is clearly, no. The question is: If nature allows a perspectival slant on meaning, and if the writer's first job is to abandon prejudice and lose himself in this embarrassment of rich interpretative material provided by his characters—by the world—how then can any one be more "moral" than the others?

Gardner's claim is that the moral perspective is the "life-affirmative" one, that you shouldn't suppress Thrasymachus, which is surely immoral—you must at least accept his report on the Real as a truth of his orientation (even this may be more than Gardner might have granted on a bad day)—but you must balance Thrasymachus with a report that simultaneously acknowledges the fact of disintegration and allows us to affirm the beliefs men have always seen as valuable: love, service, family life, sacrifice, God, and the various "good things" of life—this is, once again, no more than the idea of interpretative completeness, the philosophical (and moral) duty of presenting an aesthetic vision that, to the best of our ability, embodies as many perceptions as possible in a fiction, slighting none. Surely every story says as much about the world in what it leaves out as in what it presents. For a story to be complete—responsible and moral—it must present the modern derailments of faith and reason, which lead to despair and paralysis (these stand out strikingly as departures from our expectations and, therefore, are sensational and easy to talk about), and *also* the triumphs (these merely confirm our hopes and are damned hard to dramatize). But even this account of what fiction does falls short of Gardner's idea that fiction chooses the life-affirmative vision above all the others. He asserted but he did not prove the priority of this perception, because there can be no indubitable proof for such a claim. It is more a "faith" than an argument, an appeal to hope that nags for systematic articulation, but which defies, at every turn, demonstration.

We can show through the work of Heidegger that the self knows not the world but its vision of the world, which means that consciousness humanizes every object in the universe, brings things lofty and low onto our level, gives the world *our* face, thereby lessening terror by a little, and we can show that our gaze, or "look," as Sartre calls it, makes us at home everywhere. Similarly, we can show that society and art are intersubjective affairs—a *we* relation, which emphasizes the value of community, love, and compassion—but this is as far as even the best method can take us. We cannot say that some perceptions *should* take priority over others in a fiction and still be on safe ground. To reach this conclusion we must leave behind, as

Gardner often did, the ideal of systematic thought and turn to a softer form of persuasion: namely, description, which both philosophy and fiction share as a tool for unlocking truth.

III

In 1968, when I was twenty, the dominant themes of the Black Arts Movement, the "cultural wing" of the Black Power Movement, were paranoia and genocide. The "evidence" for a black American Holocaust seemed irrefutable. On the historical side, three centuries' worth of documentation—slave narratives, new histories such as those of Stanley M. Elkins, Eugene Genovese, and Cruse's *The Crisis of the Negro Intellectual*—drove home the sense that black history was, had always been, and might always be a slaughterhouse: a form of being characterized by stasis, denial, humiliation, dehumanization, and "relative being." If you didn't believe this—couldn't *see* it—one reading of *One Hundred Years of Lynching* would nail down the fact that our ancestors were reduced to a state of thinghood, and that this was America's master plan for all nonwhite people; you had only to ask your parents and great-uncles, late at night on the back porch, about their lives, and they told, each in turn, tales of horror in the South, then the North. Richard Wright, we suspected, had not been wrong in giving his novel *Lawd Today*, a Joycean portrayal of one day in the life of Jake Jackson, the working title *The Cesspool*.

In the contemporary world, children were dynamited in black churches, militants and pacifists both were murdered in their sleep, or blown off balconies, or set up by the FBI, or imprisoned daily—it was a period when John A. Williams could write powerfully of the secret "King Alfred Plan" to contain

blacks during riots in *The Man Who Cried I Am,* when LeRoi
Jones's play *A Black Mass* and Frantz Fanon's call for catharsis
through racial war in *The Wretched of the Earth* made a strange,
warped sense; when Sam Greenlee's *The Spook Who Sat by the
Door,* a novel of pure hatred, became the most unexpected best-
seller of the early 1970s because, as one friend told me, young
blacks read it to gain recipes for insurrection. (That same
friend's right leg was blown off when he attempted to plant a
homemade bomb in the administration building at the college
we attended in 1970.) Nature did not contradict this dark
vision—every new incident, every experience, reinforced the
"truth" that if we stayed in America, if the old order of oppression could not be changed, we would one day again be in chains.
Our African friends, we learned, lived (and still live) in fear that
recolonization of the African continent was just around the corner. And so our writers responded, each novel more terrifying
then the last: portraits of black wreckage that, like an airplane
disaster, we could not turn away from, certain this was not *a*
truth, but *the* truth, though the vision sickened us and led,
finally, to paralysis.

It would be, as I have said, immoral to suppress the vision that
black being (or all Being) is, at bottom, a ghastly joke. God only
knows that when we reach Hegel's end of history and all meanings are known, this nightmarish sense that we are locked inex-
orably into victimization may be, when we look back, *the* truth;
but the social payoff of this grim perception, particularly when
it smothers all others in a fiction (or life), is, as Gardner wrote,
immoral. We are responsible for the way the world appears
before us, for its depth and richness (if we are open to others) or
its poverty (if we are not), and for the impact our vision has on
others. "Thus is each of us," says another philosopher, "thrown
back upon himself as the 'subject' of his opinions, of his experi-

ence, upon this: he has to answer for them. He is therefore the subject of 'absolute experience'—absolute in the sense that what he acknowledges as his experience and allows to be determinant for his life depends upon himself and nothing else."[10]

You see this clearly when, for example, you are no longer in your twenties and have, say, a child named Malik. There are thousands of Maliks, children of the survivors of the 1960s. They know, as is right, nothing of the racial world yet. But I know, and my wife knows, too, that our Malik must someday learn in detail the history of slavery: *his* history, with all its despair and fatalism; he must *relive* it imaginatively, play through the horrible scenarios in his mind, discover his ruins in every black life destroyed by racism, and realize, as well, that the contemporary racial world is still a Divided Landscape, a minefield replanted so often that any step he takes will, inevitably, settle on a bomb. So it was for his father. So it was for my father. Not to tell him the field is mined— to pretend that all is well—is, obviously, to let him stumble blindly into a furnace. But is this enough?—simply to show the field as dangerous? He might choose, in this event, to sit down where he is and never walk across—too many have already opted for exactly this resignation, which means we have failed as artists and philosophers and men. For the field has fewer mines than in the beginning; it is less dangerous because so many of our predecessors have walked—or tried to walk—across, thereby lessening the possibilities of annihilation. Responsible fiction discloses these triumphs as well as the failures; it offers not the certainty that racial (and human) oppression will be resolved some day soon, as Gardner states in *On Moral Fiction* (there is, from my perspective, no such certainty), but the faith that we, and our children, can survive the minefield; can, in a word, make all minefields extinct, part of what Marx once called "the prehistory of man."

To seek a "proof" for this faith in the dignity of man, to ask Gardner to demonstrate with perfect lucidity his proposition that "man is only a little lower than the angels," is as futile as asking for yet another argument for the existence of God. But, like the belief in God (metaphorical or otherwise), John Gardner's embattled notion of "moral fiction" is an ancient faith, an essentially human faith without which no writer today can hope to achieve real, lasting significance.

"Lift Ev'ry Voice and Sing"

God of our weary years,
God of our silent tears,
Thou who has brought us thus far on the way;
Thou who has by Thy might,
Led us into the light,
Keep us forever in the path, we pray.
Lest our feet stray from the places, our God, where we met
      Thee,
Lest our hearts, drunk with the wine of the world, we forget
      Thee,
Shadowed beneath thy hand,
May we forever stand,
True to our God,
True to our native land.

I n the 1950s, in a little African Methodist Episcopal church in Evanston, Illinois, I first heard our choir perform "Lift Ev'ry Voice and Sing." If memory serves, I was an eight-year-old seated on a hard wooden bench between my parents, both wearing their go-to-meeting best, and I remember asking my mother what this particular song was about. "Just listen," she said, gently elbowing me into silence as the choir sang James Weldon Johnson's words, her voice filling suddenly with the sort of respect she reserved for things hymnal and holy. "*This*," she informed me, "is the Negro national anthem."

This, her tone said, is *important*.

Mom's explanation that Sunday morning, and her reaction, initially brought me more confusion than clarity. Didn't we, as Americans, already *have* a national anthem? And why, I wondered, did my mother, a bibliophile with the soul of an actress, a woman who was wonderfully ironic, occasionally cynical, and capable at times of devastating scorn for whatever she saw as hypocritical and phony, all but stand up and salute when this lay's last lines alchemized the air? Its simplicity was deceptive. In a way I could not unlock forty years ago, my mother was saying that it was necessary for me to understand this poem if I wanted to grasp something essential about her, my father—and myself.

Looking back, I believe now that her affection for this ineluctable work, which celebrated its hundredth birthday on February 12, 2000, consisted partly of a profound appreciation for its perennial, much-honored place in black culture, and partly of her deeply felt gratitude for the towering figure, the (Harlem) Renaissance man, who produced it as, in his own words, "an incidental effort, an effort made under stress and with no intention other than to meet the needs of a particular moment."

James Weldon Johnson is best known for his poetry, his stewardship of the National Association for the Advancement of Colored People, and his classic novel about the perils of passing for white, "The Autobiography of an Ex–Colored Man" (first

published anonymously in 1912, then reissued with his authorship acknowledged in 1927). But the spirit of his remarkable
life, influential aesthetics, and formidable political legacy is as
fully contained in "Lift Ev'ry Voice and Sing" as in his major literary and social contributions.

If we wish to experience this generation-spanning poem as
our predecessors did, give it as a gift to our children and carry it
whole into the new century, then I suspect we must revisit often
Johnson's achievements and the values and vision bequeathed to
us by our ancestors who were born just a heartbeat after the
abolition of slavery.

But one quickly discovers that Johnson's multidimensional
career resists brief recitation because he was blessed to live in a
time when black Americans believed they could do *anything*—
and did *everything*—regardless of the obstacles white people
placed in their way. (Indeed, Johnson's upbringing was so positive, he says, that he developed "an unconscious race-superior-
ity complex.") He was born in 1871 in Jacksonville, Florida, to a
self-educated father who was headwaiter at the St. James Hotel
and a mother who taught at Stanton Public School for Blacks.
While attending Atlanta University, Johnson himself taught the
children of former slaves; he wrote in his autobiography, *Along
This Way* (1933), that this experience "marked the beginning of
my knowledge of my own people as a 'race,'" and it no doubt
influenced his lifelong devotion—as a man of letters, educator,
and political activist—to "the folk."

Sometimes it seems as if we are looking at the biography of
two men, or perhaps three, when we discover that Johnson and
his musician brother, Rosamond, were, once they teamed up with
Bob Cole, remarkably successful songwriters for hit Broadway
shows ("The Maiden With the Dreamy Eyes," "My Castle on the
Nile," "Under the Bamboo Tree," "The Congo Love Song");

that he read law books in his leisure time and after some twenty months of doing this became the first black person to pass the Florida bar exam; that during his graduate study at Columbia University he began *The Autobiography of an Ex–Colored Man,* then completed it while serving as the United States consul in Venezuela (1906–9) and consul to revolution-racked Nicaragua (1909–12); that he ran the editorial page of *The New York Age,* a black, pro–Booker T. Washington newspaper; and that, as field secretary of the NAACP, he increased that organization's branches from 68 to 310. Later, in 1920, Johnson became the NAACP's first black general secretary and lobbied Congress for two years for the passage of the Dyer Anti-Lynching Bill, which passed in the House but failed in the Senate.

A luminous life, yes—a cornucopia of creativity. After a decade at the NAACP, after writing the important cultural study *Black Manhattan* (1930), editing landmark Harlem Renaissance works such as *The Book of American Negro Poetry* (1922), and publishing volumes of verse, Johnson accepted the Adam K. Spence Chair of Creative Literature at Fisk University. His restless intellect, elegant, gentleman's charm, and protean talents finally ended in an automobile accident while he was vacationing in Maine on June 26, 1938.

It was early in Johnson's life, during his years as principal of the Stanton School in his hometown, that he composed "Lift Ev'ry Voice and Sing" when he was asked to give an address for celebrating Lincoln's birthday. "I began preparing," he wrote, "but I wanted to do something else. . . . I talked over with my brother the thought I had in mind, and we planned a song to be sung as a part of the exercises. We planned, better still, to have it sung by schoolchildren—a chorus of 500 voices."

In Johnson's brief account of the song's creation, it was a hesitant muse that came to him and he groped his way through the opening. "I got my first line: Lift ev'ry voice and sing. Not a startling line; but I worked along, grinding out the next five." He gave the first stanza to Rosamond to set to music, then without pen or paper, "I paced back and forth on the front porch, repeating the lines over and over to myself, going through all the agony and ecstasy of creating." By the time he reached the final, spiritually drenched stanza, he said, "I could not keep back the tears and made no effort to do so."

"Lift Ev'ry Voice and Sing" was all he'd hoped it might be and fit the young Johnson's nascent aesthetics, which emphasized the fusion of Western forms with black content in order to conjure a new, universal vision of humanity. "I at once recognized the Kiplingesque touch in the two longer lines (of the last stanza); but I knew that in the stanza the American Negro was, historically and spiritually, immanent, and I decided to let it stand as it was written."

With their assignment for the Stanton School completed, the Johnson brothers, never ones to rest on their laurels, quickly moved on to other projects and let, as he wrote in his autobiography, "both the song and the occasion pass out of our minds." But it is one of the delicious ironies of an artistic life that frequently the work a creator hopes will be his finest achievement—or his legacy—winds up in history's dustbin while the "lesser" assignment he did in a day, without looking back, becomes the gift that captures a people's American odyssey and dreams for a century. "The schoolchildren of Jacksonville kept singing the song," he later realized. "Some of them became schoolteachers and taught it to their pupils." Within two decades it was de rigueur, "pasted in the backs of hymnals and the songbooks used in Sundays schools, Y.M.C.A.'s," and it was "sung in schools and churches throughout the South and in other parts of the country." Johnson, who lived to hear it "fervently sung" even by white students at Bryn Mawr College, confessed, "We wrote better than we knew."

The song's greatest boost surely came when "Lift Ev'ry Voice and Sing" was adopted by the NAACP (early in this century it was popularly known as the Negro National Hymn), a fact that guaranteed its wide distribution and longevity, but also might have contributed to its insouciant reception by some blacks in the last three decades of the post–Civil Rights era when the NAACP was seen as bourgeois, old-fangled, and corny by younger, more militant activists. One hears, for example, far more references these days to the seven principles of Kwanza than to the Negro National Hymn—in fact, the very word *Negro* in its title dates it as a pre-1960s document.

However, this song accomplishes the unlikely feat of transcending the age-old antinomies of integrationism vs. black nationalism, and left vs. right. It wears quite well, one decade after another, because in some thirty-odd highly compressed lines Johnson invokes the "gloomy past" of America's 244 years as a slave state (1619 to 1863), acknowledging not only this horror that brought a fledging nation to the Civil War, but also "the blood of the slaughtered," the victims of the middle passage and the Peculiar Institution whose lives, sacrifices, and struggle for liberation must never be forgotten. But notice this: "Lift Ev'ry Voice and Sing" does not morbidly dwell on that "dark past," like a sick man fingering his wounds, or see it as defining for the future; it does not catalog in mind-numbing detail every act of evil and dehumanization visited upon people of African descent, for blacks in Johnson's generation (such as W. E. B. Du Bois) were forward-looking, full of pride and faith in their own efficacy and genius. No, while the "chast'ning rod" is remembered—vividly by blacks in 1900—that past is not paralyzing. Rather, those who sang these words realized they had at last "come to the place for which their fathers sighed" though the challenges and dangers they faced as a group were far from over.

They knew, those who kept this song alive, that America was their "native land," indeed, that its history from the colonial period through Reconstruction was patently inconceivable without their influential presence in the country's economy, culture, and politics. In point of fact, they were a new people combining the promise of both the Old World and this brash, constitutional republic—"omni-Americans," in the writer Albert Murray's view. Yet in its last heartfelt lines we, as a people, are urged to stay "in the path" of morality and dignity, to fight on in the name of freedom but not to lose our souls in that secular quest, to fulfill the covenant handed to us by our predecessors and remain as God-fearing as the ancestors we honor "lest our hearts, drunk with the wine of the world, we forget Thee."

My mother, I believe, knew these idealistic stanzas spoke—and would continue to speak—directly to "the souls of black folk." And she was, as usual, right in hinting that if I wanted even a rudimentary understanding of what empowered my father to sometimes work three jobs in the 1960s to support his family, what shored up my great-uncle, a general contractor, to build churches and residences for black people all over the North Shore area, and what kept her own mother "in the path," working indefatigably for the well-being and future of her daughter and grandchild, then I—like those who had come before me—was obliged to sing this beautiful song, too. As a boy, I did. And forty years later, the song is still being sung in schools and churches, especially in the South. Even my daughter, Elizabeth, who is now twenty-one, can recite the song, which she was taught while attending a predominantly white elementary school.

In his preface to *The Book of American Negro Poetry,* James

Weldon Johnson stated, with a syncretism that must have pleased Ralph Ellison: "What the colored poet in the United States needs to do is something like what Synge did for the Irish; he needs to find a form . . . expressing the imagery, the idioms, the peculiar turns of thought and the distinctive humor and pathos, too, of the Negro, but which will also be capable of voicing the deepest and highest emotions and aspirations, and allow of the widest range of subjects and the widest scope of treatment."

In his rich contributions, especially "Lift Ev'ry Voice and Sing," elder Johnson gave Americans, black and white, that rarest of literary gifts—a song worthy of singing for a century.

An American Milk Bottle

Under a glass globe in my living room there is a remnant of my family's four centuries of history on the North American continent. I'm sure everyone who has visited my home must feel it is the strangest of heirlooms, an indecipherable piece of the American past, a tissue of time and forgotten lives. On it I often perform a private hermeneutics, peeling away its layers of meaning as one would a palimpsest. I try to imagine (as archaeologists do with tools from Pompeii or shards of pottery from the Incas) the African-American world of hope, struggle, heroism, and long-deferred possibilities that background this eighty-year-old object.

What rests mysteriously under glass is a thick, cloudy milk bottle, very scarred, that bears in relief the inscription *One Pint. This Bottle Property of and Filled by JOHNSON DAIRY CO., Evanston, Il. Wash and Return.*

The venerable Johnson who owned that bottle was my late great-uncle William. He was born in 1892 in rural South Carolina at the end of Reconstruction, near the little town of Abbeville, and just three years before Booker T. Washington's Atlanta Compromise address (and the publication of H. G. Wells's *The Time Machine*). His people lived close to the land. They farmed, spent their winters hunting, and produced everything they needed. Their water came from a well. Answering nature's call in the middle of the night meant a lonely walk outside to a foul-smelling outhouse, one's feet stepping gingerly to avoid snakes. They put their children to work at age five, making them fetch things for the adults and older children as they worked. In their daily lives nothing came easily or was taken for granted, and I am convinced that as a boy Uncle Will was mightily influenced by Booker T. Washington's famous program of self-reliance and his "philosophy of the toothbrush" (that cleanliness and meticulousness came in all things personal and professional). That, and perhaps Thoreau's challenging boast in *Walden:* "I have as many trades as fingers."

Like many black people who migrated to the North after World War I, he traveled to Chicago and settled in Evanston, a quiet suburb, bringing with him nothing more than a strong back, a quick wit, and a burning desire to succeed against staggering racial odds during the era of Jim Crow segregation. In Evanston, he discovered that white milk companies did not deliver to blacks. Always an optimist, a man who preferred hard work and getting his hands dirty to complaining, building to bellyaching, Uncle Will responded to racism by founding the Johnson Dairy Company, an enterprise that did very well, thank you, delivering milk each morning to black Evanstonians until the Great Depression brought his company to an end.

When that business failed, Uncle Will worked on a construction crew until he learned the ropes, then he started his second venture, the Johnson Construction Company, which lasted into the 1970s and was responsible for raising churches (Springfield

Baptist Church), apartment buildings, and residences all over the North Shore area—places where today, long after my great-uncle's death in 1989 at the age of ninety-seven, people still live and worship their God. In fact, once this second business took off, he was able to promise his brothers in the South jobs for their sons and daughters if they came north. My father accepted his offer and met my mother shortly after relocating to Evanston, which began the chain of causation that leads fifty-four years later to this meditation of how being an American has shaped my life as a novelist, short story writer, literary critic, philosopher, college professor, and professional cartoonist. (For example, my great-uncle is portrayed in chapter 7 of my last novel, *Dreamer*, as the fictitious black contractor Robert Jackson, whose architectural triumphs are inescapable in Evanston.)

Put simply, I grew up in a town where every day I saw or entered buildings that were produced by the ingenuity, sweat, and resourcefulness of my great-uncle's all-black construction crew, which once employed my father and uncles. And so, as a child, I never doubted—not *once*—the crucial role my people have played since the seventeenth-century colonies in the building of America on *all* levels—the physical, cultural, economic, and political. (On my mother's side, I can trace our family back to Jeff Peters, a New Orleans coachman born around 1812.) Growing up in Evanston, and attending schools integrated since the 1930s, I knew—thanks to my parents, elders, and teachers— that American democracy was a "work-in-progress," as well as an invitation to struggle (as I believe Benjamin Franklin once phrased it): an open-ended experiment in freedom, which, like a torch, was passed from one black generation to the next for its refinement and realization. My elders taught me that racism was atavistic, destined for the trash heap of human evolution, and *beneath* anyone who truly understood the real spirit of America.

As for Will Johnson, well this: I remember him as a bald, dark-skinned, potbellied, suspender-wearing family patriarch (a role my father later assumed) who had a pew reserved just for him in our AME church (he tithed heavily), watched the evening news on his black-and-white TV as if it were the oracle of Delphi (every victory during the Civil Rights Movement made him cheer the progress blacks were making in the 1950s and early 1960s), and loved to see his brother's kids and his great-nephews and -nieces come over for dinner in the two-story apartment building he had designed and built himself (he lived, naturally, on the top floor; he rented the first floor to a beauty parlor and barbershop, and he had his office, filled with maps, blueprints, and mysterious [to me] surveying equipment, in the basement). I remember him once singing to me the nifty jingle he created for his milk company. To this day I kick myself for having forgotten it. But I thank whatever powers that be for delivering to me that lonely milk bottle, which was sealed inside the wall of a building in downtown Evanston in the thirties (whoever had it *didn't* "wash and return"). A white photographer who collected curios discovered it when the building was being remodeled in 1975; he kept it and ultimately returned it to me as a gift in 1994 in exchange for a signed copy of my novel *Middle Passage* after I gave a commencement address at Northwestern University (they first asked President Clinton, but when he didn't reply, they asked me), one covered by the photographer, who, when I mentioned my great-uncle, thought to himself, "Say, I *have* that bottle at home!"

Whenever I walk through my living room, passing Uncle Will's milk bottle, I can hear the urgency that entered his voice when he counseled his great-nephews and -nieces to "Get an education. That's the most important thing you can do. Lacking that is the only thing that slowed me down." He understood—

and made *us* see through his personal example—that while black people had endured often mind-numbing oppression, America was founded on principles, ideals, and documents (the Declaration of Independence and the Constitution) that forced it to be forever self-correcting. That, he knew, was the ground that nurtured black Americans. The opportunities denied him would be there for us, he said. But *only* if we were educated and hardworking.

His vision of America, I later learned, is shared by most, if not all, the recent African, Russian, and Asian immigrants to this country that I've been privileged to meet and converse with. I did not fully appreciate the way foreigners view the positive features of American life, or see that it echoed the beliefs of my own family, until I went away to college and met a journalism major, a Ghanaian student named Fortunata Massa, who in the late 1960s said to me, "The thing I like most about America is that no matter what you want to learn, there is someone here who can teach it to you."

With those words my African friend summed up nicely the life of this native son. (And well might he have added other virtues of American life, such as this nation's support for research that leads to almost weekly discoveries in science and technological innovations; a political system the rest of the world admires; and a healthy promotion of competition that urges us always to be the best we can be.)

In elementary school my talent was for drawing. Writing I did for fun. I've kept a diary, then a journal, since I was twelve; and I published my first two short stories in 1965 in my high school newspaper's literary supplement. But it was drawing that fired my imagination and brought the greatest praise from my teachers. At age fourteen, I declared to my parents that I intended to be a cartoonist and illustrator, a fact that alarmed my father, who was concerned that this impractical decision might ruin my financial future. In his gravest voice, he told me, "Chuck, they don't let black people *do* that." I knew, of course, that he was wrong. My father only had a fifth-grade education (unlike my mother, who had finished high school and was a voracious reader who belonged to three book clubs) so he knew nothing of black artists such as the great political cartoonist Ollie Harrington; E. Simms Campbell, whose work appeared in *Esquire* and *Playboy*; Morrie Turner; or George Herriman, the creator of *Krazy Kat*. (Few people, in fact, knew Herriman was black because all his life he passed for white.) My father's words, conditioned by his Jim Crow childhood, prompted me to fire off a letter to a New York cartoonist I'd read about in *Writer's Digest*, Lawrence Lariar. He was the cartoon editor of *Parade* magazine in the 1960s, a former Disney studio "story man," editor of the annual *Best Cartoons of the Year*, and the author of more than a hundred books, some of them bestselling mystery novels. I told him what my father had said. Within a week Lariar mailed me a spirited reply: "Your father is *wrong*. You can do whatever you want with your life. All you need is a good teacher." To shorten a long story, Lawrence Lariar, a liberal Jewish man (he changed his last name in the forties) who frequently infuriated his neighbors by inviting black artists to his Long Island home, where he instructed them, became my teacher. (My dad, after seeing Lariar's letter, backed off and paid for my lessons.) Two years later I was publishing illustrations for the catalog of a Chicago company that sold magic tricks, and I won two awards in a national competition, sponsored by a journalism organization, for high school cartoonists. Over the next seven years, between 1965 and 1972, I published more than a thousand cartoons and illustrations; two books of comic art, *Black Humor* (1970) and *Half-Past Nation Time* (1972); and while earning a bachelor's degree in journalism at Southern Illinois University, I created, hosted, and coproduced an early, nationally televised PBS series called *Charlie's Pad* (1970) on which I taught others how to draw—the series ran on public TV stations around the country and Canada for about a decade. The best of this juvenilia has been anthologized and can be seen in Paul Mandelbaum's *First Words: Earliest Writing from Favorite Contemporary Authors* (1993) and in John McNally's *Humor Me: An Anthology of Humor by Writers of Color* (2002).

The insight of Fortunata Massa and my great-uncle was proven again when, in 1970, I began seriously writing novels, producing six in two years before I decided I needed to find a good teacher, one who would understand my desire to explore and expand the twentieth-century tradition of American philosophical fiction. As luck would have it, as I was finishing a master's degree in philosophy and starting my seventh novel, *Faith and the Good Thing*, the late novelist and writing teacher John Gardner, himself a philosophical writer, became my mentor, providing me with brilliant literary guidance and friendship from 1972 until his death in a motorcycle accident ten years later. As a teacher for twenty-six years, I know—as I know nothing else—that since the 1960s the availability of knowledge is the single greatest feature of American democracy, one that empowers and liberates its citizens.

It is a gift I have never taken for granted, not after promising my great-uncle that, yes, sir, I would "get an education." I relied on this virtue of Yankee life when in 1967 I began training in the Chinese martial arts at a *kwoon* in Chicago, then at other schools in New York, San Francisco, Seattle, and co-directed with a friend our own Choy Li Fut kung fu studio for ten years; when I earned a doctorate in philosophy at the State University of New York at Stony Brook, devoting my dissertation, *Being and Race: Black Writing Since 1970*, to the creation of a phenomenological aesthetic for black fiction; and, finally, when—after receiving a MacArthur Fellowship five years ago—I decided to deepen my life's long devotion to Buddhism by learning Sanskrit, not at a university but instead by studying the holy texts of Hinduism and Advaita Vedanta in the original Devanagari script with a Vedic priest who lives in Portland, Oregon, and offers private instruction. As Fortunata put it, *whatever* you want to learn, there is someone in America who can teach it to you. Yet with this freedom comes a footnote: because we enjoy such liberty, we are obliged all our lives to give in even greater measure to others.

So I've always seen my American life as an adventure of learning and growth and service. In this country no individual or group, white or black, could tell me *not* to dream. Or censor me. Or prevent me from laboring until those dreams of artistic creation and self-improvement became reality. Some tried, of course, but in America I knew that our passions define our possibilities. Sometimes when I'm working late at night and walk from my second-floor study downstairs to the kitchen for a fresh cup of tea, I see his milk bottle on an end table, and I try to imagine how Will Johnson must have looked, early in the morning before sunrise, carrying clinking bottles like this down empty, quiet streets from one Negro family's doorstep to another, hustling to get ahead, to carve out a place for himself and his loved ones against the backdrop of the New Deal and a world careening toward war. I wonder how tightly the dreams of this tall, handsome, industrious black man were tied to these tiny pint containers. Did other black men tell him he was foolish to try competing with the white milk companies? Did he stay up nights wondering, like any entrepreneur (or artist), if he might fall on his face with nothing to show for his sweat and sacrifices except spilled milk? If so, then that was just all right. For America guaranteed that he would have the chance to dream again.

Notes

Reading the Eightfold Path

1. *Buddhist Mahâyâna Texts*, trans. E. B. Cowell, F. Max Müller, and J. Takakusu, www.sacred-texts.com/bud/sbe49/index.htm (April 22, 2002).
2. *Ibid.*, Book XIV, p. 1.
3. Alan W. Watts, *The Way of Zen* (New York: Pantheon Books, 1957), pp. 91–92. Compare the classic exchange of Zen poems by Shen-hsiu and Hui-neng. Shen-hsiu's poem says:

> *The body is the Bodhi Tree;*
> *The mind is like a bright mirror standing.*
> *Take care to wipe it all the time.*
> *And allow no dust to cling.*

According to legend, Hui-neng's poem, which follows, trumped Shen-hsiu's in terms of understanding the Dharma and led to his becoming a Buddhist Patriarch:

> *There never was a Bodhi Tree,*
> *Nor bright mirror standing.*
> *Fundamentally, not one thing exists.*
> *So where is the dust to cling?*

NOTES

4. The twelve links in the chain are: (1) *Ignorance* gives rise to: (2) *Volitional action,* which gives rise to: (3) *Conditioned consciousness,* which produces: (4) *Name and form,* which leads to: (5) *The six bases* (the five senses and mind), which produce: (6) *Sense impressions,* which gives rise to: (7) *Feelings,* which then generate: (8) *Desire or craving,* which creates: (9) *Attachment,* which leads to: (10) *Becoming,* which gives rise to: (11) *Birth,* which leads to: (12) *Old age and death.* From John Snelling's *The Buddhist Handbook: A Complete Guide to Buddhist Schools, Teachings, Practice, and History* (New York: Barnes and Noble Books, 1991), p. 61.

5. Cowell, Müller, and Takakusu, *op. cit.,* Book XIV, p. 1.

6. Stephen Batchelor, *Alone With Others: An Existential Approach to Buddhism* (New York: Grove Weidenfeld, 1983), p. 39.

7. *Numerical Discourses of the Buddha: An Anthology of Suttas from the Anguttara Nikaya,* trans. and ed. by Nyanaponika Thera and Bhikku Bodhi (California: AltaMira Press, 1999), p. 65.

8. *The World Book Encyclopedia* (Chicago: Field Enterprises, 1956), vol. 2, p. 1041.

9. Maurice Walshe, *The Long Discourses of the Buddha* (Boston: Wisdom Publications, 1995), pp. 348–49.

10. *The Shambhala Dictionary of Buddhism and Zen,* trans. by Michael H. Kohn (Boston: Shambhala Books, 1991), p. 63.

11. Snelling, *op. cit.,* p. 46.

12. Gunapala Dharmasiri, *Fundamentals of Buddhist Ethics* (Antioch, Calif.: Golden Leaves Press, 1989), p. 109.

13. "Two foundations of twentieth-century physics—quantum theory and relativity theory—both force us to see the world very much in the way a Hindu, Buddhist, or Taoist sees it": Fritjof Capra, *The Tao of Physics* (New York: Bantam Books, 1984), pp. 4–5.

14. The following statement has been attributed to Albert Einstein: "The religion of the future will be a cosmic religion. It should transcend a personal God to avoid dogma and theology. Covering both the natural and the spiritual, it should be based on a religious sense arising from the experience of all things natural and spiritual as a meaningful unity. Buddhism answers this description. . . . If there is any religion that could cope with modern scientific needs, it would be Buddhism."

15. Walshe, *op. cit.,* p. 348.

16. Thich Nhat Hanh, *Living Buddha, Living Christ* (New York: Riverhead Books, 1995), pp. 133–35.

17. Thich Nhat Hanh, *Being Peace* (Berkeley, Calif.: Parallax Press, 1987), p. 45.

18. *The Martin Luther King Jr. Companion*, ed. by Coretta Scott King (New York: St. Martin's Press, 1993), p. 94.

19. *Ibid.*, p. 91.

20. Hanh, *Living Buddha, Living Christ*, p. 11.

21. Consider these words of the Buddha from the *Anguttara Nikaya:* "It is impossible, O monks, and it cannot be that a person possessed of right view should regard any formation as permanent. . . . It is impossible, O monks, and it cannot be that a person possessed of right view should regard any formation as a source of happiness. . . . It is impossible, O monks, and it cannot be that a person possessed of right view should regard anything as a self. But it is possible for an uninstructed worldling to regard something as a self." From *Numerical Discourses of the Buddha*, pp. 37–38.

22. In his outstanding work *Nonduality* (New York: Humanity Books, 1998), David Loy provides a concise account of *sunyata.* "It comes from the root *su*, which means "to swell" in two senses: hollow or empty, and also full, like the womb of a pregnant woman. Both are implied in the Mahayana usage: the first denies any fixed self-nature to anything, the second implies that this is also fullness and limitless possibility, for lack of any fixed characteristics allows the infinite diversity of impermanent phenomena," p. 50.

23. A comparison of Buddhism's doctrine of dependent origination and Whitehead's project of developing a metaphysics based on quantum theory would make for a very useful study, since for Whitehead, who abandons the subject-object mode of thinking, entities are epochal units of becoming interconnected in a universe that is itself a process of becoming, and every actual entity is present in every other actual entity.

24. Alex Kennedy, *The Buddhist Vision* (York Beach, Me.: Samuel Weiser, 1987), pp. 170–71.

25. Paul Carus, *Gospel of Buddha*, (Tucson: Omen Communications, 1972), p. 34.

26. "Because we label objects in the world with nouns we come to think of them as unchanging entities—isolated, interacting only by a system of mechanical exchanges. We even think of ourselves in this same way": Kennedy, *op. cit.*, p. 82.

27. *The Zen Teachings of Huang Po: On the Transmission of Mind*, trans. by John Blofeld (New York: Grove Press, 1958), pp. 81–82.

28. *World of the Buddha,* ed. by Lucien Stryk (New York: Doubleday, 1968), p. 343.

29. Hanh, *Living Buddha, Living Christ,* p. 106.

30. *Ibid.,* p. 183.

31. "I am composed of form and matter, neither of them will perish into nothingness, as neither of them came into being out of nothingness. Every part of me then will be reduced by change into some other part of the universe, that again will change into another part of the universe, and so on forever. And as a result of such a change, I too now exist, and those who begot me existed, and so forever in the other direction": Marcus Aurelius, *Meditations,* trans. George Long (Roslyn, N.Y.: Walter J. Black, 1945), p. 50.

32. "Take away your opinion, and there is taken away the complaint, 'I have been hurt.' Take away the complaint, 'I have been hurt,' and the hurt is gone": *ibid.,* p. 35.

33. Dharmasiri, *op. cit.,* p. 135,

34. *Teachings of the Buddha,* ed. by Jack Kornfield (Boston: Shambhala Books, 1993), p. 101.

35. Consider his words in light of Matthew 19:17, "Why callest thou me good? There is none good but one, that is God." And John 14:10, "Believest thou not that I am in the Father and the Father in me? The words that I speak unto you I speak not of myself, but the Father that dwelleth in me, he doeth the works."

36. "Consider that before long you will be nobody and nowhere, nor will any of the things exist which you now see, nor any of those who are now living. For all things are formed by nature to change and be turned and to perish in order that other things in continuous succession may exist": Aurelius, *op. cit.,* p. 129.

37.
> *Suffering alone exists, none who suffer;*
> *The deed there is, but no doer thereof;*
> *Nirvana is, but no one seeking it;*
> *The Path there is, but none who travel it.*

From Alan Watts, *The Way of Zen* (New York: Vintage Books, 1957), p. 56. Consider also the Zen poem:

> *To write something and leave it behind us,*
> *It is but a dream.*
> *When we awake we know*
> *There is not even anyone to read it.*

38. *The Diamond Sutra & the Sutra of Hui-Neng,* trans. A. F. Price and Wong Mou-lam (Boston: Shambhala Books, 1990), p. 35.

39. *Ibid.,* p. 53. Compare this to Aurelius' counsel, "Return to your sober senses and recall yourself. When you have roused yourself from sleep and perceived that they were only dreams which troubled you, then in your waking hours look at the things about you as you looked at the dreams." Aurelius, *op. cit.,* p. 62.

40. Walshe, *op. cit.,* p. 348.

41. Dharmasiri, *op. cit.,* p. 45.

42. Isshu Miura and Ruth Fuller Sasaki, *The Zen Koan: It's History and Use in Rinzai Zen* (New York: Harvest Books, 1965), p. 36.

43. Shantideva, *A Guide to the Bodhisattva's Way of Life,* trans. Stephen Batchelor (Dharamsala: Library of Tibetian Works & Archives, 1979), pp. 114–15.

44. Walshe, *op. cit.,* p. 348.

45. Carus, *op. cit.,* pp. 106–8.

46. Martin Heidegger, *Being and Time,* trans. John Macquarrie and Edward Robinson (New York: Harper and Row, 1962), p. 213.

47. *The Shambhala Dictionary of Buddhism,* p. 121.

48. All information on Sanskrit here is drawn from "Sanskrit and the Technological Age: Mathematics, Music, and Sanskrit" and "The Yoga of Learning Sanskrit," by Vyaas Houston, *Devani: The Language of the Gods* (New York: The American Sanskrit Institute, n.d.), pp. 1–8 and 17–27.

49. David P. Barash, "Buddhism and the 'subversive' science," *The Chronicle of Higher Education,* February 23, 2001, pp. 13–14.

50. Houston, *op. cit.,* p. 38.

51. *Ibid.*

52. *Ibid.,* p. 20.

53. *Astavakra Samhita,* by Swami Nityaswarupananda (Calcutta: Advaita Ashrama, 1969), p. 100.

54. It is also interesting to note that the Sanskrit word for "form," *rupam,* also means "beauty."

55. For example, see the final line in Book VI, verse 11, of *The Bhagavad Gita,* trans. Winthrop Sargeant (Albany: State University of New York Press), p. 282.

56. Walshe, *op. cit.,* p. 348.

57. Dharmasiri, *op. cit.,* pp. 27–28.

58. Literally, "eight-thousand-line wisdom perfection" sutra.

59. *The Perfection of Wisdom,* selected and trans. R. C. Jamieson (New York: Viking Studio, 2000), pp. 65–67.

60. *The Zen Teachings of Huang Po,* p. 20.

61. Jamieson, *op. cit.,* p. 71.

62. *The Three Pillars of Zen,* ed. Philip Kapleau (Boston: Beacon Press, 1967), pp. 301–13.

63. *Shambhala Dictionary of Buddhism,* pp. 106–7.

64. Kapleau, *op. cit.,* p. 301.

65. *Ibid.,* p. 311.

66. *Ibid.,* p. 313.

67. Consider this in light of Matthew 6:27: "Which of you by taking thought can add one cubit unto his stature?"

68. "You have lived as a part. You shall disappear in that which produced you; rather, you shall be received back into the creative principle by a transformation": Aurelius, *op. cit.,* p. 36.

69. Chogyam Trungpa Rinpoche, "The Decision to Become a Buddhist," *Shambhala Sun,* May 2001, pp. 28–33. The Dalai Lama, I should note, prefers that we see ourselves as "tourists" in this world, a point he explains in *Ethics for the New Millennium* (New York: Riverhead Books, 1999).

70. Batchelor, *op. cit.*

71. H. Saddhatissa, *Buddhist Ethics* (New York: George Braziller, 1970), p. 140.

72. Poem by P'ang-yun, cited in Watts, *op. cit.,* p. 133, and Snelling, *op. cit.,* p. 139.

73. Walshe, *op. cit.,* p. 348.

74. Kennedy, *op. cit.,* p. 123.

75. *A Testament of Hope: The Essential Writings and Speeches of Martin Luther King, Jr.,* ed. James M. Washington (New York: Harper-Collins, 1991), pp. 224–26.

    It is instructive to compare the Eightfold Path to a document used during the Birmingham campaign, entitled "Commandments for Volunteers," which civil rights activists signed. This decalogue said: "I hereby pledge myself—my person and body—to the nonviolent movement. Therefore I will keep the following commandments: (1) Meditate daily on the teachings and life of Jesus; (2) Remember always that the nonviolent movement seeks justice and reconciliation—not victory; (3) Walk and talk in the manner of love, for God is love; (4) Pray daily to be used by God in order that all men might be free; (5) Sacrifice personal wishes in order that all men might be free; (6) Observe with both friend and foe the ordinary rules of courtesy; (7) Seek to perform regular service for others and for the world; (8) Refrain from the violence of fist, tongue, or heart; (9) Strive to be in good spiritual and bodily health; (10) Follow the directions of the movement and of the captain on a demonstration." These commandments can be found in my novel *Dreamer* (New York: Scribner, 1998), pp. 91–92.

76. *The Dhammapada*, trans. Irving Babbitt (New York: New Directions, 1965), p. 3.

Compare Babbitt's rendering of these opening lines to those of Thanissaro Bhikkhu (Geoffrey DeGraff) in his translation of the *Dhammapada* (Barre, Vt.: Dhamma Dana Publications, 1998), p. 1:

> *Phenomena are preceded by the heart,*
> *ruled by the heart,*
> *made of the heart.*
> *If you speak or act*
> *with a corrupted heart,*
> *then suffering follows you—*
> *as the wheel of the cart,*
> *the track of the ox*
> *that pulls it.*

77. *The Dhammapada, op. cit.,* p. 6.
78. *Ibid.,* p. 8.
79. Obviously, I side with the Husserlian account of consciousness, expressed in his famous formula "Consciousness is always consciousness *of* something," where the subject (*noesis*) and object (*noema*) are interdependent, both arising simultaneously to make experience itself possible. This rather Kantian interweaving of the Transcendental Ego and the phenomenal world provides a useful starting point for discussing the Buddhist doctrine of No-self.
80. Think of this in light of Aurelius' advice: "Men seek retreats for themselves, houses in the country, seashores and mountains; and you too are wont to desire such things very much. But this is altogether a mark of the common sort of man, for it is in your power, whenever you shall choose, to retire into yourself. For nowhere with more quiet or more freedom from trouble does a man retire than into his own soul, particularly when he has within him such thoughts that by looking into them he is at once perfectly tranquil; and this tranquility, I am sure, is nothing but the good ordering of the mind.

NOTES

Constantly then grant yourself this retreat and refreshment." Aurelius, *op. cit.,* p. 33.

81. Walshe, *op. cit.,* pp. 348–49.
82. *Ibid.,* p. 350.
83. Saddhatissa, *op. cit.,* p. 74.
84. Kennedy, *op. cit.,* p. 199.
85. Swami Budhananda, *The Mind and Its Control* (Calcutta: Advaita Ashrama, 1978), pp. 98–99.
86. "If you strive to live only what is really your life, that is, the present—then you will be able to pass that portion of life which remains for you up to the time of your death, free from perturbations, nobly, and obedient to your own deity within": Aurelius, *op. cit.,* p. 126.
87. Kennedy, *op. cit.,* p. 57.
88. Arun Venugopal, "Breathing-in-peace tour," *The Seattle Times,* May 4, 2002, p. A-11.
89. Walshe, *op. cit.,* p. 49.
90. Dharmasiri, *op. cit.,* p. 123.

On the Book of Proverbs

1. Kenneth T. Aitken, *Proverbs* (Philadelphia: The Westminster Press, 1968), p. 3.
2. J. Vernon McGee, *Proverbs* (Nashville: Thomas Nelson Publishers, 1991), p. x.
3. Thomas à Kempis, *The Imitation of Christ,* trans. Leo Sherley-Price (Middlesex, U.K.:Penguin Books, 1953), p. 50.
4. *The Dhammapada,* trans. Irving Babbitt (New York: New Directions, 1965), p. 18.

Uncle Tom's Cabin

1. Abraham Lincoln, from Jane Smiley's introduction to *Uncle Tom's Cabin* (New York: Modern Library, 2001), p. xxii. Smiley gives no citation for the quotation. However, in *The World Book Encyclopedia* (Field Enterprises, 1956), the entry for Stowe gives a slightly different version of the quotation: "So this is the little woman who made the big war."
2. The Stono Rebellion took place on September 9, 1739, in South Carolina.

3. Henry Adams, from John A. Garraty's *The American Nation: A History of the United States* (New York: Harper & Row, 1966), p. 178.
4. Charles Dickens, from *Uncle Tom's Cabin* (New York: Modern Library, 2001), p. 641.
5. James Baldwin. An excerpt from "Everybody's Protest Novel" (*Partisan Review* 16, June 1949); the quotation used appears in *Uncle Tom's Cabin* (New York: Modern Library, 2001), p. 641.

On *Kingsblood Royal*

1. All quotes from Sinclair Lewis's essay "A Note About *Kingsblood Royal*" are taken from *The Man from Main Street*, Harry E. Maule and Melville H. Crane, eds. (New York: Random House, 1953), pp. 36–41.
2. Mark Shorer, *Sinclair Lewis: An American Life* (New York: McGraw-Hill, 1961), p. 748.
3. All material from Robert E. Fleming is from "*Kingsblood Royal* and the Black 'Passing' Novel," in *Critical Essays on Sinclair Lewis*, Martin Bucco, ed. (Boston: G. K. Hall & Co., 1986), pp. 213–21.
4. *Great Negroes Past and Present*, Russell L. Adams, ed. (Chicago: Afro-Am Publishing Co., 1969), p. 122.

Progress in Literature

1. Material on the evolution of the novel is taken from Richard M. Eastman, *A Guide to the Novel* (San Francisco: Chandler Publishing Co., 1965).
2. This discussion of the short story's evolution is drawn from Eugene Current-Garcia and Walton R. Patrick, eds., *What Is the Short Story?* (Glenview, Ill.: Scott, Foresman and Co., 1974).

A Phenomenology of *On Moral Fiction*

1. John Gardner, *In the Suicide Mountains* (New York: Alfred A. Knopf, 1977), p. 91.
2. John Gardner, "Amber (Get) Waves (Your) of (Plastic) Grain (Uncle Sam)," *The New York Times*, October 29, 1975, op-ed page.
3. John Gardner, *Nickel Mountain* (New York: Alfred A. Knopf, 1973), p. 302.

4. Don Edwards and Carol Polsgrove, "A Conversation with John Gardner," *The Atlantic* 239, no. 5 (1977): 44.

5. Alfred Schutz and Thomas Luckman, *The Structures of the Life-World,* trans. Richard M. Zaner and H. Tristram Englehardt Jr. (Evanston, Ill.: Northwestern University Press, 1973), p. 60.

6. The full explanation for this technique, as it applies to phenomenology, is provided by Herbert Spiegelberg in "Phenomenology Through Vicarious Experience," in Edwin W. Strauss, ed., *Phenomenology: Pure and Applied* (Pittsburgh: Duquesne University Press, 1964).

7. Maurice Merleau-Ponty, *The Visible and the Invisible,* ed. Claude Lefort, trans. Alphonso Lingis (Evanston, Ill.: Northwestern University Press, 1968), p. 49.

8. Maurice Merleau-Ponty, *Adventures of the Dialectic,* trans. Joseph Bien (Evanston, Ill.: Northwestern University Press, 1973), p. 53.

9. *Ibid.,* pp. 138–39.

10. Ludwig Landgrebe, "The Problem of the Beginning of Philosophy in Husserl's Phenomenology," in *Life-World and Consciousness,* ed. Lester E. Embree (Evanston, Ill.: Northwestern University Press, 1972), p. 49.

Acknowledgments

First, I would like to thank my superb editor, Ileene Smith, for conjuring an order out of these many essays and articles written over nearly twenty years. Thanks is also due to critic John Whalen-Bridge for his valuable responses to first drafts of a few essays here on the Dharma; to my Sanskrit teacher, Aja Thomas, a Vedic priest, for his four years of outstanding instruction; to Helen Tworkov for publishing two of these essays in *Tricycle:The Buddhist Review* and several of my Zen cartoons in *Buddha Laughing;* to Drs. Richard Salomon and Collett D. Cox at the University of Washington for checking my Devanagari script; and, of course, to my wife, Joan, and two children for providing me with a rich family life that, as the late Eknath Easwaran put it, "gives us countless opportunities every day for expanding our consciousness by reducing our self-will or separateness."

ABOUT THE AUTHOR

Charles Johnson was born in 1948 in Evanston, Illinois. He is currently the S. Wilson and Grace M. Pollock Endowed Professor of English at the University of Washington in Seattle. Johnson has written four novels: *Faith and the Good Thing* (1974), *Oxherding Tale* (1982), *Middle Passage* (1990), and *Dreamer* (1998); and two short story collections: *The Sorcerer's Apprentice* (1986) and *Soulcatcher* (2001). His nonfiction books include *Being and Race: Black Writing Since 1970* (1988), *Black Men Speaking* (1997), *Africans in America: America's Journey Through Slavery* (1998), and *King: The Photobiography of Martin Luther King Jr.* (2000), as well as two collections of comic art, *Black Humor* (1970) and *Half-Past Nation Time* (1972). Dr. Johnson has also written numerous screenplays for film and television. He has received many awards, including an NEA grant, Guggenheim and MacArthur Fellowships, and an Academy of Arts and Letters Award in Literature. Johnson won the National Book Award for *Middle Passage* in 1990.